History and Architecture of Edina, Minnesota

History and Architecture of Edina, Minnesota

William W. Scott, A.I.A., and Jeffrey A. Hess

Setter, Leach & Lindstrom, Inc.,
architects, engineers and planners
Minneapolis, Minnesota

City of Edina
Edina, Minnesota

Additional copies of this book may be ordered from:

City of Edina
4801 West 50th Street
Edina, Minnesota 55424

Copyright © 1981 by the City of Edina. All rights reserved.

Library of Congress Catalog Card Number: 80-68450
International Standard Book Number: 0-9605054-0-7
Printed in the United States of America

Contents

Foreword

This is a report on buildings of historical and architectural significance in Edina, Minnesota. It represents the results of a historic building survey of the entire community conducted for the Heritage Preservation Board of the City of Edina in 1979.

Like many of the suburbs surrounding central cities, Edina is often regarded as a post-World War II phenomenon, and, indeed, a great deal of development that has occurred in the city dates from that period. However, Edina is more than a product of the 1950s and 1960s. The city has a long and impressive history that spans over 120 years. This history is reflected in its architecture, which includes a significant number of buildings from the pre-World War I era.

We hope that the publication of this survey will focus attention on these structures, creating an awareness of Edina's architectural heritage and providing a basis for further preservation planning in our community.

By its very nature, a work of architecture is a kind of public monument. However, most of the buildings discussed in these pages are also private residences. We trust that those who use this book as a guide to sight-seeing in Edina will in turn be guided by a respect for the privacy of others.

FOSTER W. DUNWIDDIE
Chairman

Heritage Preservation Board
Edina, Minnesota
June 30, 1980

Acknowledgments

The authors wish to express their appreciation to the following people who assisted in the preparation of this book.

Edina City Council

James Van Valkenburg, Mayor; A. Charles Bredesen; C. Wayne Courtney; Frederick S. Richards; June A. Schmidt.

Edina Heritage Preservation Board

Foster W. Dunwiddie, Chairman; Maryanne Herman; Thomas R. Martinson; Paul Mucke; Betty Paugh; Gordon Stuart; Frank A. Thorpe.

Administrative Assistance

Ken Rosland, Edina City Manager; Harold Sand, Planner; Jeannie Davis; Ralph E. Johnson; Robert James Lunieski; Jo Taylor Provo; June Regan; Patrick Zaimes.

Archival Assistance

Dorothy Burke, Minneapolis Public Library; Shirley G. Dunwiddie, Edina Historical Society; Alan Lathrop, Northwest Architectural Archives, University of Minnesota; Elaine Murray, Hennepin County Historical Society; Bonnie Wilson, Minnesota Historical Society.

Private Collections

Paul and Mary Carson, Foster W. Dunwiddie, Stewart J. and Ruth G. McIntosh, E. Dudley Parsons, Jr., Samuel Thorpe, Jr.

Design and Production

Greg Fern.

Graphics

Carol Berdan, Jeffrey Frush.

Photography

Robert Novak, Peter A. Rand, Jeffrey A. Hess.

Editing

Mary Ann Nord.

The authors also wish to thank the many past and present Edina residents who so generously shared their time and memories.

This publication was made possible by a grant from the United States Department of the Interior, Heritage Conservation and Recreation Service, Federal Preservation Fund, and the Minnesota Historical Society's state grants-in-aid program.

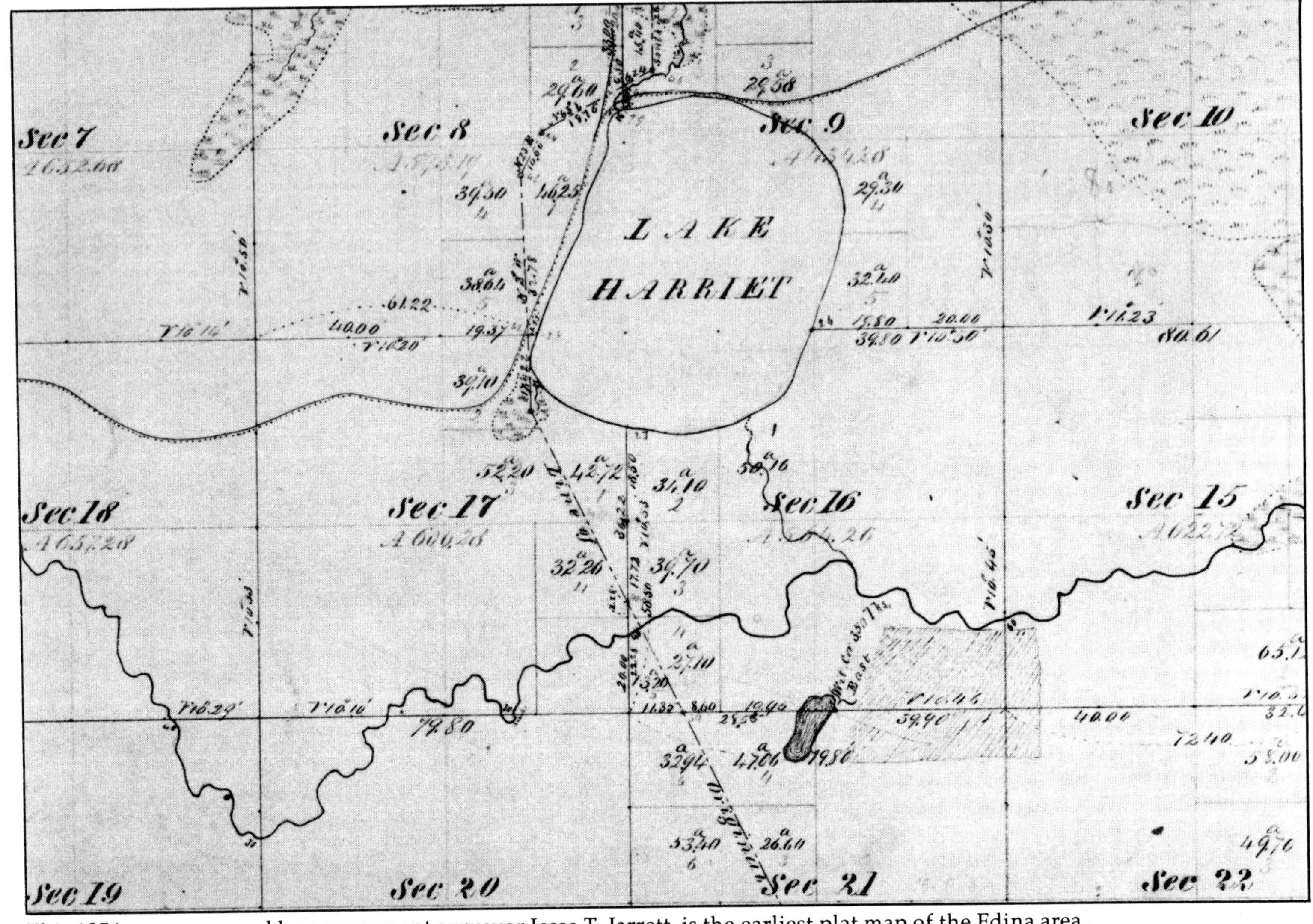

This 1854 map, prepared by government surveyor Jesse T. Jarrett, is the earliest plat map of the Edina area. Minnehaha Creek runs across the bottom. The vertical section line on the left is now France Avenue South.

Picnickers waded in Minnehaha Creek on the James A. Bull farm at the turn of the century. The Bull farm was located just south of West 50th Street.

Sand Castles on France Avenue: An Introduction

In August 1853, Jesse T. Jarrett walked a straight line across the countryside of southeastern Minnesota Territory. A surveyor for the United States Land Office, Jarrett was laying out the west line of Section 20, Township 28, North Range 24, West 4th Principal Meridian. In his field notes, he described the landscape:

> Brown's Creek 30 links wide, runs N.E. swift current, high banks and gravelly bed . . . . Surface rolling: Soil 2nd rate. Timber South of Creek scattering, Bur & Black Oak. North of Creek, Heavy Black Oak & Aspen. Undergrowth Oak, Aspen, Plum Hawthorn & Grape.[1]

Today the map of Edina bears little resemblance to Jarrett's survey description. Jarrett's section line is now a major thoroughfare known as France Avenue South. Brown's Creek, no longer swift and deep, is called Minnehaha Creek. The once rolling fields and woodlands have been carved into hundreds of streets and mantled with thousands of homes.

Yet there are residents of Edina who remember an earlier landscape.

Aldora Cornelius Hallaway has lived most of her life in a farmhouse at 6101 France Avenue South. Her parents, Adolph and Catherine Cornelius, built the house in 1910, the year before she was born. "Sometimes when I drive home at night and see the lights of Southdale and all those houses," Aldora explains, "I can't help but think how things have changed. Why, I can remember building sand castles in the middle of France Avenue when I was a little girl. My parents scolded me for playing in the street. But it seemed perfectly safe. There was hardly any traffic.

"We had about thirty-two acres of land off France Avenue. We raised vegetables for the wholesale merchants in Minneapolis — parsley, carrots, cauliflower, green beans. During the summers, we had a hired man who lived in an old two-room farmhouse just behind our house. My parents had lived there when they were first married. It's torn down now. We used some of the lumber to build our garage.

"As far back as I can remember, there were quite a few houses on France Avenue. But the land behind our house was perfectly clear. Between France and Beard avenues, and between 60th and 62nd streets, there was nothing but a large hayfield. It was empty except for four big walnut trees. My older brother George was an aviation buff, and he owned an airplane. He used the hayfield as an airport. The only thing he had to watch out for was those four walnut trees. The trees are gone now. We cut them down when we sold the land in the early 1950s. Taxes were getting so high."[2]

Bill Hoffman also remembers the face of rural Edina. "My family moved to Edina in 1928 when I was five years old. At first we lived in a farmhouse off Normandale Road. It's the south end of the golf course now. When I was a youngster, I worked for a man named Pauley who owned a threshing rig. We used to do the farms off 70th Street. In those days there were some big farms in that neighborhood. And pheasants. My God, there was pheasants! I can

Browndale Avenue, 1909.

This 1951 photograph shows the Haeg farmhouse (lower right) on its original site at the intersection of Valley View Road and Wooddale Avenue.

remember kicking up a cloud of pheasants near 67th and France. There must have been two hundred of them.

"The land's not the only thing that's changed. A lot of the houses have changed too. When I was growing up, my family went to the Edina Baptist Church at 5501 France Avenue. The building's still there, but you'd never know it was a church. The steeple's been taken down, and it looks like just a regular house now. My own home is another example. When I got married in 1951, I bought the old Haeg farmhouse which used to sit on the corner of Wooddale Avenue and Valley View Road. The land had just been bought by a developer, so I moved the house to 6233 Peacedale Avenue. At that time people didn't move houses much. Everyone thought I was crazy. To tell the truth, I thought I was crazy too. But I love that old house. I wouldn't want to live anyplace else."[3]

Other longtime residents of Edina, such as Lewis Jones and E. Dudley Parsons, Jr., have stories to tell about other parts of the city. All these reminiscences share a common theme. They reveal how the cityscape of modern Edina has resulted from the interplay of many processes: changing land use, new construction, demolition, building relocation, and the adaptive reuse of older structures.

This book attempts to analyze these processes in order to describe the richness and variety of Edina's architectural heritage. Data has been drawn from surveyor's maps, municipal and county archives, newspaper files, interviews with past and present Edina residents, and field inspections of the city's standing structures.

Feeding chickens on the Bull farm in Edina Mills, c. 1905.

Raking leaves in Braemar Hills, 1980.

From Farmyards to Backyards: A Brief History

Suburbanites, especially in newly developed subdivisions, frequently combine a pioneer's attitude toward history with a city dweller's sense of place — which is to say, history begins with their own arrival and is measured in terms of building density. "The history of Edina? What history?" asks a young woman who grew up in the Indian Hills region during the 1960s. "When we first built our house, there was hardly anything out here." Judged from such a perspective, Edina is indeed lacking in historical depth. At least 80 percent of the homes in the community were built after 1950; entire neighborhoods bear the unmistakable stamp of the 1960s and the 1970s.[1] Yet Edina is not simply the creation of the post-war building boom. Its origins reach back into Minnesota's territorial days, and even its suburbanization is of venerable lineage.

Before the Village of Edina was incorporated in 1888, the area was part of Richfield Township, which once embraced nearly all of the territory west of the Mississippi River to Hopkins and south of Lake Street to Bloomington.[2] The settlement of the township began in the early 1850s. When the first government surveyors platted the region in 1853-54, they noted that in the western half of the township "a large portion of the land is claimed, and some of it improved," while in the eastern half "at least four-fifth[s] . . . is claimed and one-half . . . settled on."[3] By 1860 three major community centers had emerged: Richfield Mills (West 54th Street and Lyndale Avenue South), Waterville Mills (West 50th

Street and Wooddale Avenue), and Cahill Settlement (West 70th Street and Cahill Road).[4] In varying degrees, each of these communities helped shape the course of modern Edina.

Richfield Mills was the largest and most prosperous of the three communities. Its preeminence resulted at least partly from its advantageous location. Straddling the Bloomington Road (now Lyndale Avenue South) near Minnehaha Creek, Richfield Mills had both an excellent waterpower site and direct access to Minneapolis. Occupying the geographic center of Richfield Township, it also served as the seat of local government. During the 1860s the community contained a custom grist mill, a store, a school, a blacksmith shop, and two churches.[5] Although the site of Richfield Mills lies outside the boundaries of Edina, its influence on the early settlement patterns of the area is not to be ignored. As the commercial and administrative center of the township, it undoubtedly stimulated the growth of neighboring sections, including the area that was to become eastern Edina.

With the success of Richfield Mills, a second milling community soon developed a few miles west on Minnehaha Creek. At its center stood Waterville Mills, erected in 1857 by Jacob Elliot, Richard Strout, Levi M. Stewart, and Joseph Cushman. After two changes in ownership, the mill was purchased in 1869 by Andrew Craik, a Scottish immigrant from Canada who renamed the enterprise "Edina Mills," after his native city of Edinburgh. Although the early Edina Mills community was overshadowed in commercial importance

Scottish miller Andrew Craik named his grist mill "Edina Mills" after his native city of Edinburgh.

Edina Mills, built in 1857, stood beside Minnehaha Creek, just east of the Browndale Avenue bridge. The mill was demolished in 1932.

EDINA MILLS

CRAIK & SON,

Manufacturers and Wholesale Dealers in

Oat Meal, Pearl Barley, Flour,

FEED AND GRAIN.

PRODUCE AND COMMISSION

219 FIRST AVENUE SOUTH,

MINNEAPOLIS, MINN.

Like most custom millers, Craik received as a fee one-tenth of the grain ground at his mill. To market his flour and feed, he opened an outlet store in downtown Minneapolis.

by its Richfield counterpart, it nevertheless served as an important business and cultural center for the surrounding countryside. By the mid-1870s it contained an Episcopalian church, a schoolhouse, and a Grange hall.[6]

The third major community in early Richfield Township was Cahill Settlement. Established in the 1850s by Irish immigrants, the community found its focal point at the junction of Cahill Road and West 70th Street. On the southeast corner of this intersection, the settlers erected a one-room, frame schoolhouse in 1864. The school also served as a meeting place for St. Patrick's Catholic Church until a separate sanctuary was built on the southwest corner in 1884.[7]

Since religious differences were often the basis of social cleavage in the mid-nineteenth century, it is not surprising that the Catholic Cahill Settlement and the Protestant Edina Mills formed distinct communities with separate school systems. The two sections were united, however, by a common rural lifestyle and agricultural economy. During the early years, farms were largely subsistence operations, producing limited amounts of vegetables, corn, small grains, and livestock. After this initial "pioneer" period, Cahill Settlement and Edina Mills seem to have followed somewhat different courses. While diversified farming remained strong in Cahill throughout the nineteenth century, some farmers in Edina Mills turned to more specialized agriculture. Jonathan T. Grimes, for example, established an apple orchard on his 160 acres in the northeastern Edina Mills area. Grimes's neighbor George W. Baird raised Merino sheep; another neighbor, H. F. Brown, was known for his pure-bred cattle.[8]

By 1886 the area that two years later was to become the Village of Edina contained about 485 people and 85 residential and commercial buildings.[9] Most of these structures were located in the immediate vicinity of major thoroughfares, now known as Cahill Road, France Avenue South, Interlachen Boulevard, Valley View Road, Vernon Avenue, West 50th Street, and West 70th Street. Patterns of building density offer a clue to population dispersal during this period. If the Edina area were to be divided into approximately equal quadrants, the northeast sector (including Edina Mills) would account for almost 45 percent of the buildings. The other three quadrants (with Cahill Settlement comprising the southwest sector) would equally share the remaining structures. The greater concentration of buildings in Edina Mills probably signified a larger population. Even after the mill suspended operations in the late 1880s, the area remained a significant social and trading center.[10]

This schoolhouse was built in 1888, the year Edina became a village. Located on the site of the present Edina City Hall, the building served School District No. 17 until the mid-1920s.

The founding of the Village of Edina in 1888 was an obvious assertion of local identity. At the same time, it was a reaction against the encroachments of the Minneapolis city limits. During the 1880s Minneapolis experienced unprecedented residential growth. At the beginning of the decade, the city's limits barely reached beyond Lake Street. By the end of the decade, they extended as far south as West 54th Street, absorbing even the old Richfield Mills community.[11] The swiftness of metropolitan expansion was facilitated by state law, which permitted annexation of unincorporated township territory without a vote of township residents. In incorporated areas, however, annexation required a mandate of the electorate.[12] Annexation was a mixed

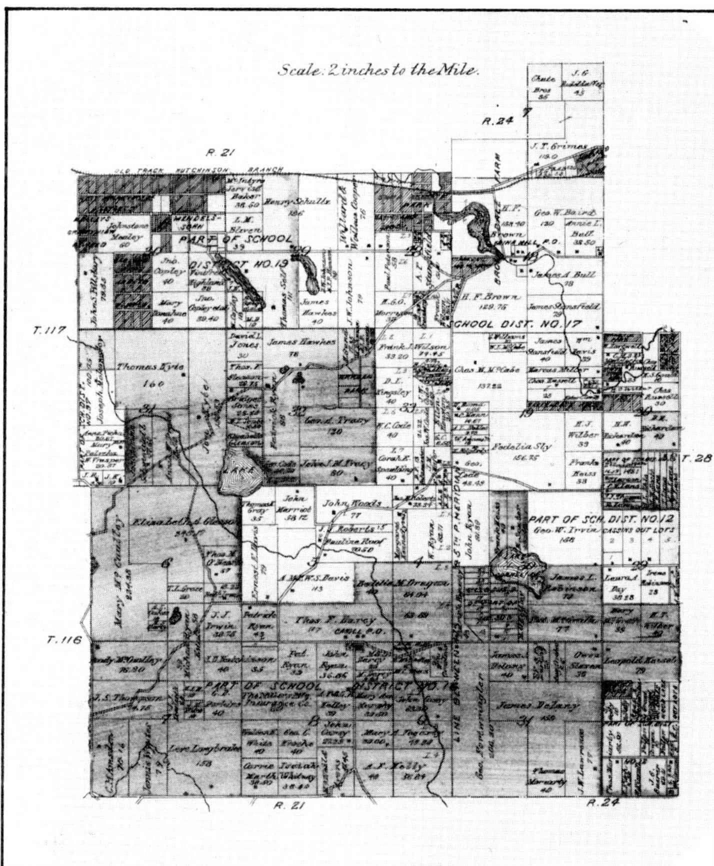

This 1898 plat map of Edina reveals the basic features of an agricultural village. There are few major thoroughfares, and most landowners hold parcels of at least forty acres.

blessing. Although it held the promise of greater public services and profitable land transactions, it also threatened to increase property taxes and disrupt traditional rural life-styles.

To resolve the issue of annexation, residents of Richfield Township gathered at the polls on December 12, 1888, to vote on incorporation. Separate elections were held in the eastern and western halves of the township. The eastern half voted to remain unincorporated. Residents of the western half voted overwhelmingly in favor of forming a village. After considering such names as "Hennepin Park" and "Westfield," the new village decided to retain the name of the old milling community and called itself "Edina."[13]

Incorporation as a village ensured Edina's political autonomy. But it proved an uncertain defense against the effects of metropolitan expansion. The Depression of 1893 put an end to the building boom of the 1880s. However, with an upturn in the economy after the turn of the century, new construction resumed. As early as 1904 the Edina Village Council found itself grappling with the bewildering new phenomenon of "suburbanization." As the council's minutes record:

> Whereas large numbers of pursons [*sic*] have acquired and are acquiring small tracts of land ranging from one acre to five or ten acres within the corporate limits of the Village of Edina, and are demanding of the Village Council of said village the acquiring and opening of numerous streets . . . to accommodate such owners and;
>
> Whereas to acquire and open and improve such streets as are so demanded at the expense of said

village will entail . . . heavy burdens of taxation on large numbers of people resident and owning land in said village who are in no manner benefitted by such proposed improvements, and;

Whereas such improvements will ordinarily benefit few people and but small amounts of land, Therefore,

Be it resolved by the Village Council of the Village of Edina that hereafter when new streets are condemned and opened . . . the cost thereof . . . shall be assessed against the property benefitted by such improvement. . . .[14]

This was only a prelude. When in 1905 the Twin City Rapid Transit Company announced plans to establish streetcar service through Edina, suburbanization began in earnest. That same year the Grimes family, with a Minneapolis real estate broker, C. I. Fuller, platted part of the old Jonathan T. Grimes homestead into building lots and opened the new subdivision of "Morningside." The *Minneapolis Journal* boldly heralded the new suburban development:

NICKEL LIMIT IS PUSHED WESTWARD
HARRIET LINE EXTENSION OPENS
NEW SUBURBAN PROPERTY

Part of the Old Jonathan Grimes Farm
Has Already Been Platted in Acre Tracts
for Those Who Will Like to Live
Far from the Maddning [*sic*] Throng.

One of the first incidental benefits accruing from the improvement and extension of the Lake Harriet trolley line is the platting of an acre home colony, for suburban residences just outside the city limits, by C. I. Fuller. This immediately follows the announcement that the Twin City Rapid

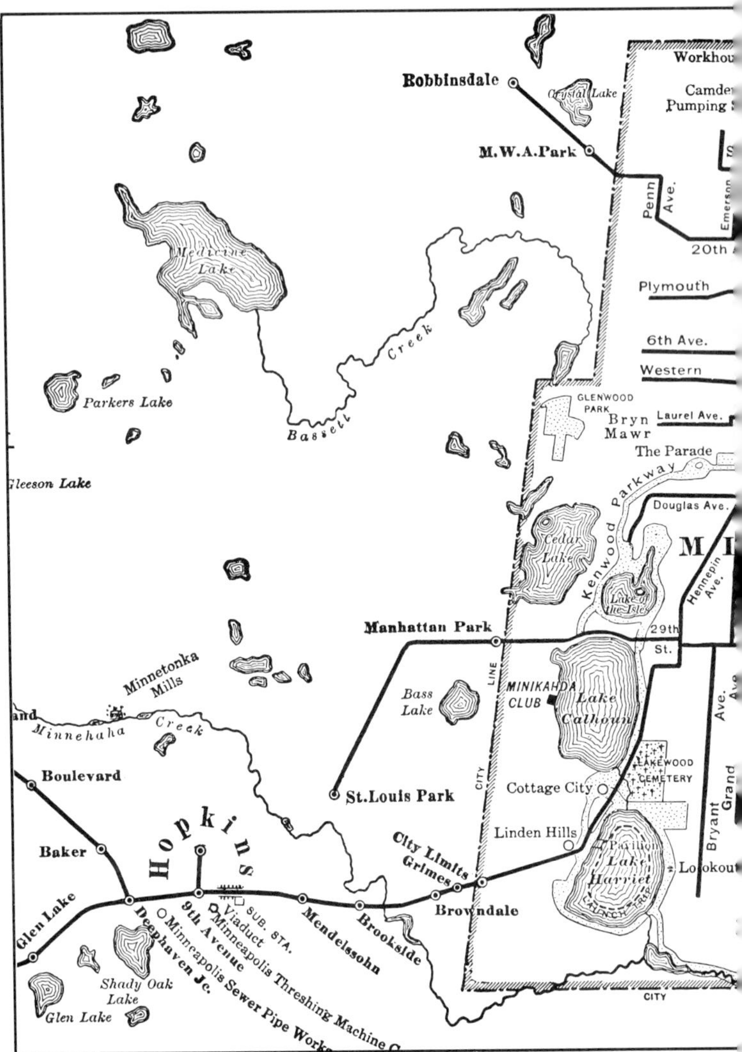

The first streetcar stations in the Morningside area were locat along West 44th Street at France Avenue South, near the Grin House, and on Browndale Avenue.

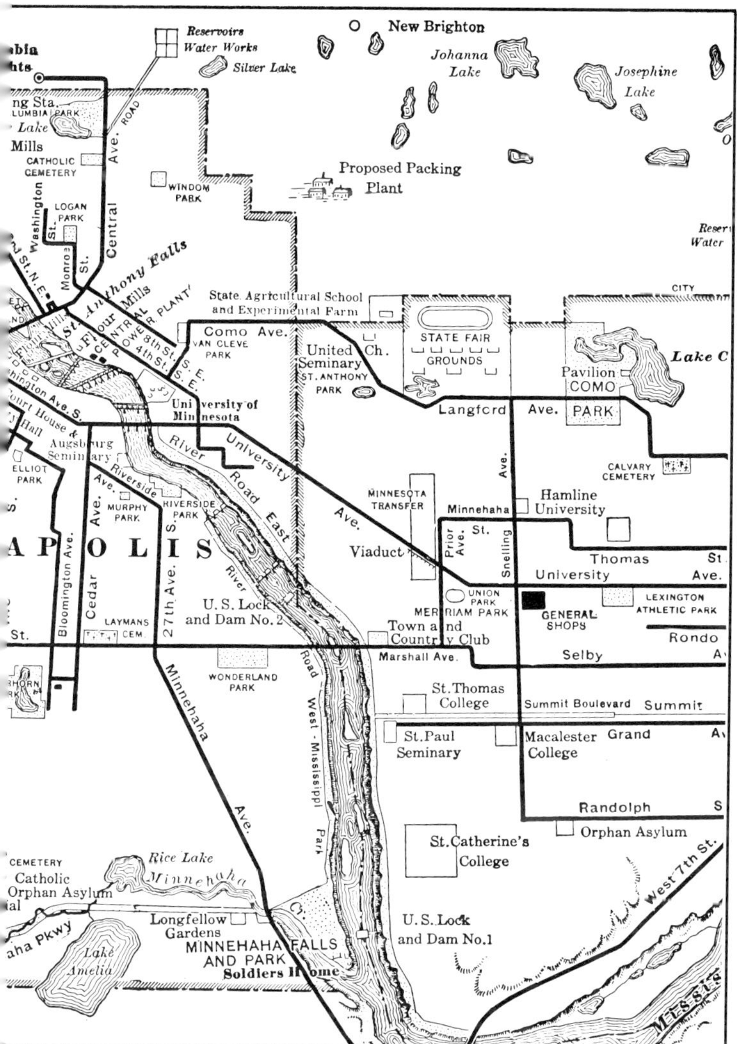

Transit Company will change the present Harriet loop from Sheridan Avenue to the city limits at France Avenue, ten blocks to the west . . . .

Mr. Fuller's new district, Morningside, is composed of sixty-nine lots, 100 by 300 feet each, to cost from $250 to $1,000. The district lies between Forty-second and Forty-fourth streets and will be crossed by three new avenues, Alden, Scott, and France. Electric cars will stop at three stations adjacent to the Fuller property. Tenants living outside the city limits will have low taxes and at the same time only 5-cent carfare to town.[15]

Morningside was immediately successful, attracting mainly white-collar workers who commuted to their jobs in Minneapolis. Subsequent platting increased the Morningside area until it included almost all the territory north of Sunnyside Road. By 1920 Morningside contained about 500 of Edina's 1,833 people.[16] E. D. Parsons, a teacher at Minneapolis's West High School who settled in Morningside in 1903, has described the rural attractions that brought so many city dwellers to Edina's first suburban development: "We balanced our living cost with the products of garden, orchard and pasture and gave our boys a natural playground, and provided all of us stimulating and useful labor."[17]

But Morningsiders were not content with mere pastoral charms. They insisted on having streetlights, sidewalks, and paved roads – extravagant notions as far as the farmer-dominated Village Council was concerned. Throughout the 1910s, council meetings witnessed an elaborate choreography of pitched battles between the Morningside Improvement Association and the rural council members. Finally on September 18, 1920, Morningsiders gathered at the Odd Fellows Hall at 4388 France Avenue South to discuss the formation of a new village.[18] The case for secession had already been clearly stated in the *Lake Harriet News*:

> It is time that Morningside emerged from its chrysalis stage and became a recognized entity instead of being a revenue appendix of 8,500 acres of pasture, woodland, and cornfield. Is there any reason why an intelligent, wide-awake and up-to-date community should not administer its own affairs instead of being governed by "absentee treatment"? We have young men in Morningside — attorneys, bankers, realtors, engineers, contractors and other business and professional men, who are admirably equipped to administer its affairs, whom we would meet face to face daily and who would listen to our requests for service in a sympathetic and respectful attitude.[19]

The final vote on secession was close, with 148 in favor and 131 opposed. On November 27, 1920, the new Village Council of Morningside met with the Village Council of Edina to "discuss a division of the spoils," amicably agreeing to split outstanding assets and liabilities at the end of the fiscal year.[20]

The secession of Morningside did not return Edina to the rural simplicity of the nineteenth century. Although the village had lost its most visible and vocal suburban development, several other areas of new residential construction remained within municipal limits. These included Brookside Avenue north of Interlachen Boulevard and the subdivisions of West Minneapolis Heights and Mendelssohn bordering the streetcar line in north-

Looking north along France Avenue South in Morningside, 1933.

No. 259 (Revised 1926) Miller-Davis Co., Minneapolis

200 24

Village of Edina

Hennepin County, Minnesota

OFFICE OF VILLAGE RECORDER

Building Permit

IN CONSIDERATION OF The statements and representations made by ....

in..........application therefor duly filed in this office, which application is hereby made a part hereof, PERMISSION IS HEREBY GRANTED To said..........as owner to Build chicken house ....a building described as follows: kind of construction
(build, erect, install, add to, alter, repair, move, wreck, as the case may be)

front or width in feet 16; side or length in feet 30; height in feet..........; number of stories..........; contents..........; cubic feet..........square feet, upon that tract of land described as follows: Lot 23 Block 13; plat or addition Fairfax

which tract is of the size and area specified in said application.

This permit is granted upon the express conditions that said owner and his contractors, agents, workmen and employees, shall comply in all respects with the ordinances of the Village of Edina; that it does not cover the use of public property, such as streets, sidewalks, alleys, etc., for which special permits must be secured; and that it does not cover the following: ....
(Electrical work, plumbing, heating, plastering, etc., if such there be.)
for which special permits must be secured.

Given under the hand of the President of said Village Council and its corporate seal and attested by its Recorder this 14 day of Sept 1930

Attest:

Village Recorder. President of Village Council.

Barns and chicken coops were familiar sights in Edina as late as the 1940s.

western Edina.[21] The rise of new construction paralleled a gradual decline of the Edina farming community itself. As Edina historian Paul Hesterman has observed:

> In 1898, Edina was virtually covered by 40-acre and 80-acre plots, while in 1925 there were only 13 farms between 25 and 50 acres in size, and only 8 between 50 and 100 acres. The majority of farms in 1925 (41) are under 25 acres.[22]

The surrender of rural Edina to the pressures of suburbanization was finalized by a single real estate transaction in 1922. That year, realtor Samuel Thorpe of Thorpe Bros. purchased the H. F. Brown farm, comprising approximately 300 acres in the heart of the old Edina Mills community. On this site (roughly bounded by West 44th Street on the north, Arden Avenue on the east, West 50th Street and Minnehaha Creek on the south, and Normandale Road on the west), Thorpe promised to build a "high-class" residential district unlike anything ever seen before in the Upper Midwest. And he kept his word. Modeling his venture on J. C. Nichols's Country Club District in Kansas City, Missouri, Thorpe landscaped his development with contoured streets, shade trees, parks, and an eighteen-hole golf course. He set rigid building restrictions regarding minimum valuation, construction siting, architectural style, and property maintenance. And he installed all major utility services before any of the approximately 550 building lots were placed on the market in the spring of 1924.[23]

Thorpe's Country Club District was cordially received by the Edina Village Council. Undoubtedly the council members were pleased at the prospect of not having to pay for the district's initial public improvements. Perhaps, after their experience with Morningside, they had even come to accept the inevitability of suburbanization. When Thorpe attempted to foster the secession of the district a few years later, he was opposed by both Country Club residents and the Edina Village Council.[24]

By 1930 the Country Club District contained 269 houses and over 1,000 residents — nearly one-third of Edina's total population. But the district's impact on the village is scarcely told by census statistics. The Country Club set an architectural standard for future suburban developments in the village. It led to the modernization of the West 50th Street and France Avenue South commercial district, which until the late 1920s had been an unpaved crossroads.[25] And it encouraged the Village Council to adopt principles of city planning. In 1929 Edina became the first village in Minnesota to approve a comprehensive zoning ordinance.[26]

The Country Club District also helped define the future transportation patterns of the village. Unlike Morningside, Country Club was not a "streetcar suburb." Although Thorpe's promotional brochures acknowledged the district's proximity to streetcar service, it was well understood that the executive and professional classes who settled in Country Club would depend on the automobile for transportation. When Thorpe in 1925 put a "completely equipped" model home on display, its furnishings included "a 1925 model, popular priced automobile standing at the front door."[27]

Unlike the Edina Mills area with its Country Club development, the old Cahill Settlement remained a rural neighborhood throughout the 1930s

The H. F. Brown Farm, shortly before realtor Samuel Thorpe purchased the land for the Country Club District.

Minnehaha Creek bordering the Country Club District, c. 1931.

France Avenue South and West 50th Street, c. 1945.

and 1940s. But it too experienced significant changes. By this time several of the area's original Irish families had moved on, to be replaced by a more heterogeneous population. The construction of Calvary Lutheran Church on the northwest corner of West 70th Street and Cahill Road marked the district's increasing ethnic and religious diversity.[28]

World War II virtually suspended new home construction in all parts of Edina. But with post-war prosperity, suburbanization resumed at an unprecedented pace. From 1946 to 1950, a total of 1,897 building permits were issued. And by the mid-1950s, the city's population was increasing at an annual rate of 2,500 people.[29] Although this growth rate abated somewhat during the 1960s, the decline was partially offset by the return of Morningside to its parent community in 1966.

Today Edina is a city of approximately 50,000 inhabitants in 12,400 residential structures — a staggering increase over the 5,855 residents and 1,545 dwellings of 1940.[30] Considering these statistics, it is not surprising that Edina is sometimes thought to be a "mushroom suburb" that suddenly appeared overnight. It takes imagination and a sense of history to see the city in the garb of an earlier day when it was "an agricultural village; the only settlement at the crossing of the Minnehaha Creek, where there is a post office, a mill, and a store. . . ."[31]

Wooddale School, Wooddale Avenue and West 50th Street.

A Matter of Style: Edina's Changing Architecture

When architectural historians discuss building styles, they have in mind fairly specific combinations of form, proportion, ornamentation, and materials. Most architectural styles are named for their reputed place of origin (Italianate), period of greatest popularity (Georgian), leading practitioner (Eastlake), or major idiosyncratic feature (Stick style). Like other social conventions, architectural styles rise and fall, revive and again retire, according to the dictates of popular taste.

When Edina was first settled in the 1850s, Greek Revival architecture had already begun its fall from fashion in the eastern United States. From the 1820s to the 1850s, the style had been the nation's most popular form of architecture. In the Midwest, where settlers were more concerned with breaking sod than architectural convention, Greek Revival remained in vogue until the 1870s. By that time, however, the style had been considerably diluted. The need for haste in construction to accommodate a burgeoning population, coupled with a lack of trained craftsmen and architects, resulted in the elimination of much of the detail, the elaborate, heavy entablatures, and the columned porches of the classic Greek Revival style. Finally, only the form and proportions of the style remained, typically in the guise of a low-pitched gable roof and formal placement of doors and windows.

Extant examples in Edina of this much simplified version of Greek Revival include the Cahill School

(1864), which was moved from its original location at West 70th Street and Cahill Road to Frank Tupa Park at Eden Avenue and Highway 100; the Sly House (c. 1866-1870) at 6128 Brookview Avenue; and the former Trinity Chapel (1872) at 4924 France Avenue South.[1] Although the latter two buildings have been altered, they retain the proportions and something of the flavor of the Greek Revival style.

Gothic Revival architecture was introduced to the United States in the 1830s on a wave of romanticism stimulated by the writings of such authors as John Ruskin and Sir Walter Scott. Gothic Revival attempted to recall the castle, church, or cottage of medieval Britain. Though never as prevalent as Greek Revival, it lasted well into the twentieth century. The mid-nineteenth-century version of the style is best identified by its use of steeply pitched roofs with decorative trim resembling vines curling along the gables and eaves; pointed- or lancet-arch window heads; and massive chimneys, or clusters of chimneys.

From the 1840s to the 1880s, the Italianate style replaced both Greek Revival and Gothic Revival as the favored design for residences and commercial buildings. The Italianate style is distinguished by its block-like forms topped with low hip roofs, wide eaves supported by massive decorative brackets, and elaborate hood moldings over round- or segmental-arch windows. From the 1860s to the 1880s, as the country rapidly changed from an agrarian to an industrial economy, Italianate vied with the Mansard-roofed French Second Empire style as the most ostentatious means for the growing numbers of merchants and industrialists to flaunt their new wealth.

Simplified Greek Revival: Cahill School on its original site at Cahill Road and West 70th Street, 1935.

Gothic Revival and Italianate: Grimes House, 4200 West 44th Street.

Vernacular Farmhouse: 403 Washington Avenue (above), 6125 Ewing Avenue (below).

As a recently settled community dependent on the output of its farms and small mills, Edina had little of the time, money, or skill required to produce the grand examples of Italianate and French Second Empire architecture found in more established and prosperous areas. The city's most impressive residence surviving from the period of early settlement (1850s to 1870s) is the Grimes House (1869) at 4200 West 44th Street. Although primarily Gothic Revival with its pointed-arch windows, the house also suggests the Italianate in its bay window and conspicuous brackets supporting wide eaves.

Perhaps the building most typical of Edina architecture from about 1870 to 1900 is the "Vernacular Farmhouse." This is a rectangular, clapboard-sided, frame structure, usually painted white. Additions are common; when attached to one side, they create a distinctive L-shaped appearance. The Vernacular Farmhouse essentially expresses the already simplified Greek Revival style, modified even further by a steeper pitch to the gable roof for protection against heavy snows, and by a less formal placement of windows and doors. Because the carefully studied proportions of the Greek Revival were abandoned, the Vernacular Farmhouse tends to be too high for its width. Usually a wide bay window appears on the first-floor street facade. The building has almost no decoration, with the exception of the customary turned posts on the open front and side porches.

While a number of Vernacular Farmhouses survive in Edina, many have been altered beyond recognition. Even without major structural changes, a building's original character was often greatly altered by the removal or enclosure of open porches, by the replacement of the narrow, horizontal wood siding and vertical corner boards with wide composition or metal siding, and by the relocation or redesign of windows and doors. Typical examples of the Vernacular Farmhouse are found at 6125 Ewing Avenue (c. 1893) and 5717 Blake Road (1878). Among a collection of older houses in the West Minneapolis Heights section of Edina are Vernacular Farmhouses at 303 and 319 Madison Avenue (c. 1910, c. 1893) and 307 Jefferson Avenue (c. 1910).

A variation of the Vernacular Farmhouse style, also found in West Minneapolis Heights, is the "Midwest Saltbox." This is a late-nineteenth-century adaptation of the Colonial New England Saltbox. The Saltbox is a rectangular, one-and-one-half-story or two-story, frame structure with a gable roof. Characteristically, the gable slopes steeply over a rear addition to create what New Englanders call a "cat slide" roof. Edina's most complete Midwest Saltbox, at 308 Madison Avenue (c. 1910), would fit almost unnoticed into any early Massachusetts community. Other West Minneapolis Heights examples are houses at 305 and 309 Jefferson Avenue (c. 1910).

With the exception of a style known as Eastlake, there is little evidence today in Edina of Queen Anne, Richardsonian Romanesque, Shingle, and most of the other Victorian architectural styles and substyles that flourished in the late nineteenth century. Some modest pretentions to design and decoration can be found in residences at 5 Cooper Avenue (c. 1898) and 403 Washington Avenue (c. 1893), buildings that might otherwise be classified as Vernacular Farmhouses. On both structures, the square-cornered walls of the second floor of one wing over-

Midwest Saltbox: 308 Madison Avenue.

Eastlake detailing: 5 Cooper Avenue.

Eastlake detailing: 5312 Interlachen Boulevard.

Stick style: Grange Hall in Frank Tupa Park, Eden Avenue and Highway 100.

hang the splayed corners of the first floor, a characteristic detail of the Eastlake style.

The Eastlake style derives its name from Charles Locke Eastlake, an English interior designer who advocated the abandonment of florid Victorian motifs. Although still highly ornamental in character, Eastlake buildings achieve a measure of stylistic restraint by the replacement of heavy, rounded Victorian embellishments with thinner, more lineal detailing. As seen in the second story of the house at 5312 Interlachen Boulevard (c. 1880), the American adaptation of Eastlake features a liberal use of fishtail shingles, fan-like gable-end decoration, and incised lineal detailing in the jamb and window head. The Baird House (1886) at 4400 West 50th Street, a brick-and-stone variation of Eastlake, is early Edina's largest and most impressive mansion.

Simpler and starker in form than Eastlake is the Stick style (1860s to 1890s). The key elements of this style are exposed wood structural members, such as corner posts, window and door frames, brackets, sill plates, and diagonal bracing, that project beyond the horizontal clapboard siding. These features are often oversized to provide emphatic contrast to the siding. The Grange Hall (1879), which has been moved from its original site at Wooddale Avenue and West 50th Street to Frank Tupa Park at Eden Avenue and Highway 100, is one of the rare, albeit modest, examples of this design in Minnesota.

By the 1890s, the Vernacular Farmhouse in Minnesota was being replaced by another modest style sometimes called "Midwest Square." Although found throughout the nation, this style was particularly common in the central region. Just as the

Vernacular Farmhouse seems to have evolved from the Greek Revival, the Midwest Square may be a much simplified variation of the cube-shaped, low hip-roofed Italianate. Midwest Square houses are comfortable, informal, clapboard-sided, frame structures. While the wide roof overhangs of the Italianate style remain, decorative support brackets have been removed. Unadorned, rectangular frames replace the ornate hoods over round- or segmental-arch door and window openings. Standard-sized, double-hung windows with a single pane of glass in each sash are used in place of the tall, narrow, two-paned Italianate window sash. The front porch remains, but with massive, square support posts and balustrade instead of the fussy, turned-wood elements of the Italianate style. Interior room arrangement in the Midwest Square often results in a less formal placement of window and door openings, especially at the sides and rear of the building.

Examples of the Midwest Square abound in Edina. Those at 6101 France Avenue South (1910) and 4222 Grimes Avenue (1916) represent the hip roof variation of the style. A number of Midwest Squares, such as the houses at 4315 Morningside Road (c. 1910) and 6204 France Avenue South (c. 1900), have simple gable roofs with smaller gabled dormers on each side. Though rectangular rather than square in plan, the house at 5920 Hansen Road (c. 1910) illustrates the occasional use of the gambrel roof on Midwest Squares.

At the end of the nineteenth century, Edina was still a relatively isolated rural community. Probably few village residents were immediately aware that the powerful Ecole des Beaux Arts in Paris had decreed a return to the carefully studied proportions

Midwest Square with gable roof: 6204 France Avenue South.

Midwest Square with hip roof: 4222 Grimes Avenue.

Midwest Square with Palladian windows: 4410 Curve Avenue.

English Tudor Revival: 4379 Coolidge Avenue.

and details of Greek and Roman designs. When the influence of Beaux Arts classicism eventually did reach Edina, it was in the diluted form of a general interest in historic revival styles. Among the earliest of these was the Colonial Revival style, in which such details as the Palladian window, used frequently in eighteenth-century American Georgian buildings, were applied to houses of other styles. A number of Edina residences show vestiges of this applied ornamentation, including those at 4410 Curve Avenue (1910), with its Palladian windows in the gables, and 6615 Belmore Lane (c. 1900), exhibiting a sunburst detail over the entrance. As the twentieth century progressed, Colonial Revival residences became increasingly accurate replicas, in external form and detail, of the original American Georgian, New England Saltbox, Cape Cod, and Williamsburg models.

English Tudor Revival was another of the popular early historic revival styles. It attempted to express the architecture of sixteenth- and seventeenth-century England through its use of steep gables, clustered chimneys, and exposed half-timber construction infilled by brick, stone, and stucco. English Tudor became especially popular in Edina in the 1920s and 1930s. But two early variations at 4520 West 44th Street (1913) and 4379 Coolidge Avenue (1913) are among the best examples in the city.

Although some early-twentieth-century architects found relief from Victorian excess in the controlled universe of historic revival styles, others rejected all forms of traditional expression. They attempted to establish a new architectural direction reflecting more informal life-styles, innovative building techniques, and a more harmonious integration of structure and setting. Proponents of the new architecture, such as Louis Sullivan, Frank Lloyd Wright, William G. Purcell, and George C. Elmslie, developed a style that came to be known as "Prairie School."

The same developments that inspired Prairie School architecture fostered two other styles — Craftsman and California Bungalow. Both these styles had an enormous influence on residential design throughout the country after 1900. With their emphasis on practical, easily maintained materials and efficient, informal floor plans, Craftsman and Bungalow houses were inexpensive and especially appealing to an increasingly servant-less society. The styles featured the use of stucco, wood siding, brick, field stone, stock millwork, and exposed structural systems unencumbered by decorative moldings.

In Minnesota, Craftsman houses were usually two or more stories. Bungalows, if more than one story, were designed with projecting roofs, large dormers, and deep porches to effect a one-story height. Examples of the Craftsman style in Edina are located at 4311 Morningside Road (1914) and 4330 France Avenue South (1907). Bungalows are much more prevalent in the city. There is a particularly handsome, unaltered version at 4305 Morningside Road (c. 1915). A large and more expansive example occurs at 4211 Morningside Road (1913). The diversity of materials and design in the Bungalow style is evident in the rich collection at 3920, 4006, 4010, 4012, 4014, 4016, 4018, and 4020 West 44th Street (c. 1910 - c. 1920). Especially noteworthy is the al-

Craftsman style: 4311 Morningside Road.

Bungalow style: 4305 Morningside Road.

Mission Revival: 4246 Scott Terrace (above), 4500 West 44th Street (below).

most Japanese quality of the magnificent bungalow at 4116 West 44th Street (1911).

Somewhat akin to the Craftsman-Bungalow movement was the Mission Revival style, which enjoyed a brief popularity in Minnesota during the early 1900s. This too was a style dedicated to the stripping away of superfluous architectural elements. It was also a historic revival style, which sought to reproduce in white stucco and curvilinear gables the adobe missions of the early southwestern United States. Among local examples are houses at 4311 Eton Place (c. 1905-11) and 4246 Scott Terrace (1911) in Morningside. An especially handsome example is the house at 4500 West 44th Street (c. 1910). The red tile roofs and squat corner watchtower of this house provide a gentle contrast to the stark white stucco walls and the low horizontality of the building's mass.

Although Craftsman, Bungalow, and Mission Revival styles were the rule in modest communities like Morningside, more elaborate historic revival architecture held sway in affluent developments like the Country Club District. Country Club is a veritable museum of historic revival houses. Only a lone Bungalow at 4613 Bruce Avenue (1924) and several comparatively recent houses of contemporary design interrupt the stylistic mix of approximately 550 English Tudor, English Cottage, Norman, French Provincial, American Colonial, Renaissance, and Mediterranean revivals.

Typical of the English Tudor Revival style from the 1920s and 1930s are houses at 4511 and 4600 Edina Boulevard (c. 1930) and 4517 Drexel Avenue (c. 1930). Together they exhibit the characteristic Tudor half-timbering, steep gables, and clustered chimney. Among the variations of traditional English Tudor houses is the residence at 4637 Casco Avenue (c. 1928), with its crenellated entrance wing and four-pointed-arch openings. The large two-story house at 4624 Browndale Avenue (c. 1930) blends with its neighbors through the use of equally spaced, vertical half-timbering. This feature just barely manages to disguise as English Tudor what is essentially a Prairie School house. Although the architect is unknown, the building strongly suggests the influence of Chicago architect George W. Maher.

English Tudor Revival: 4511 Edina Boulevard.

Architectural styles closely associated with English Tudor Revival are the English Picturesque and the English Cottage. While the Tudor Revival recalls the grander houses of the era of Henry VIII and Elizabeth I, the Picturesque and Cottage styles are patterned after smaller houses with a more rural, domestic character. The Picturesque and Cottage are similar styles, with the latter being reserved for buildings of more diminutive scale. Both styles emphasize steep gables, at least one side of which often swoops down to enclose a round-arch main entrance or garden gate. Structures may be of stone, stucco, or patterned brick. Especially handsome variations can be found at 4610 Drexel Avenue (c. 1936) and 4602 Moorland Avenue (c. 1930). The latter employs decorative stone trim around the round-arch entrance and on the foundation, front steps, and chimney. One of the largest and most impressive Picturesque structures in the city is the stone house at 4401

English Picturesque Revival: 4610 Drexel Avenue.

Norman Revival: 4507 Edina Boulevard.

French Provincial Revival: 4612 Moorland Avenue.

Browndale Avenue (c. 1928). Houses at 4603 Drexel Avenue (c. 1925) and 4517 Arden Avenue (c. 1930) typify a number of English Cottages throughout the Country Club District.

Because English architecture was heavily influenced by the Norman Conquest, it is not surprising that English Tudor Revival houses closely resemble the Norman Revival style. The principal distinguishing feature of Norman Revival, as seen in the particularly noteworthy example at 4507 Edina Boulevard (c. 1930), is the main entrance located in a round tower, or keep, capped with a conical roof. The house at 4608 Drexel Avenue (c. 1930) is also an example of Norman Revival architecture.

Another popular revival style of French origin is French Provincial. As the name implies, the style derives from houses of seventeenth- and eighteenth-century rural France that were more substantial than peasants' cottages, but less imposing than chateaus. French Provincial houses are identified by their hip roofs and segmental-arch windows and dormers. Because the roofs of peasant cottages were frequently thatched, architects have gone to extraordinary lengths, with varying degrees of success, to achieve the same soft, rounded effect with composition shingles. While the brick house at 4500 Moorland Avenue (c. 1936) might be described as a transitional phase between Norman Revival and French Provincial styles, the residence at 4615 Edina Boulevard (c. 1934) is a purer example of the latter. French Provincial houses at 4612 Moorland Avenue (1927) and 4614 Edina Boulevard (1927) display more sophisticated detail in the corner quoins, the broken pediments above classic doorways, and the more formal placement of windows and doors.

Mediterranean Revival, also known as Spanish Colonial, is an all-inclusive description for those houses inspired by the architecture of Spain and Mexico. The design, featuring small windows and white walls, originally evolved to accommodate a hot, dry climate. In the 1920s and 1930s, southern California adopted the style and developed a residential architecture integrating white stucco walls, flat or low hip roofs of red clay tile, small wooden or wrought iron balconies, twisted churrigueresque columns, and ornate wooden doors. The style eventually enjoyed great popularity throughout the country. Kansas City's Country Club Plaza, for example, recalls old Seville. Edina's Country Club District also has its share of Spanish motifs, as displayed in houses at 4500 Edina Boulevard (c. 1925); 4609 and 4619 Moorland Avenue (c. 1928, c. 1930); 4402, 4601, and 4604 Browndale Avenue (c. 1927, c. 1929, c. 1925); 4503 Casco Avenue (c. 1930); and 4531 Arden Avenue (c. 1935). Wooddale School (1926) at West 50th Street and Wooddale Avenue reflects a Spanish Colonial influence in its arched openings, twisted columns, and hint of curvilinear gables at building entrances.

Only a few houses in the Country Club District are designed in the Italian Renaissance mode. This style, which began in sixteenth-century Italy, was itself a revival of classical Greek and Roman architecture. The house at 4520 Casco Avenue (c. 1940?) reveals the basic features of the style: stuccoed walls; a low hip, tiled roof; and a centered doorway with classical trim. The "palazzo" at 4513 Wooddale Avenue (c. 1929) typifies the monumental character often achieved in houses of this style.

Mediterranean Revival: 4402 Browndale Avenue.

Italian Renaissance Revival: 4520 Casco Avenue.

American Colonial Revival: 4601 Casco Avenue (above), 4527 Arden Avenue (below).

The residential design that has most consistently enjoyed America's favor is the Colonial Revival. Within this style, there is a great richness and variety, ranging from Early American to Cape Cod and American Georgian. Early American is an adaptation of seventeenth-century New England residential architecture, which in turn was a continuation of medieval English domestic designs. As illustrated by the rather loose interpretation of the style in the house at 4606 Moorland Avenue (c. 1927), the most notable characteristic of Early American is the overhang of the second floor, with decorative pendants terminating the corner posts on the underside of the projection. Looking as though it could have been moved directly to Edina from Salem, Massachusetts, or Portland, Maine, the house at 4601 Casco Avenue (c. 1925) is a particularly faithful reproduction of a clapboard-sided, New England Colonial dwelling. Similarly, the brick house at 4527 Arden Avenue (c. 1936) might have been erected 150 years earlier in Tidewater Virginia. Typical of the formal, two-story American Georgian houses built in the Country Club District are those at 4520 Browndale Avenue (c. 1936), 4634 Bruce Avenue (c. 1934), and 4607 and 4613 Edina Boulevard (c. 1930).

Although this analysis of Edina's historic revival architecture has focused on the Country Club District, several of the city's other residential neighborhoods could just as effectively have been used to illustrate the discussion. Of course, the story of Edina architecture does not end with historic revival styles. After World War II, dozens of new suburban developments transformed Edina into a showcase of modern architecture. The chronicle of these more recent events, however, must be left for future architectural historians.[2] It is sufficient here to call attention to the many post-1950 buildings in Edina that have been cited for merit by the Minnesota Society of the American Institute of Architects:

St. Peter's Lutheran Church
5421 France Avenue South
Ralph Rapson, architect
1958 Merit Award

Municipal Bathhouse
Valley View Road between 66th Street and Highway 62
Shifflet, Backstrom, Hutchinson and Dickey, architects
1959 Honorable Mention

Bruce A. Abrahamson Residence
7205 Shannon Drive
Bruce A. Abrahamson, architect
1959 Merit Award

Moore Residence
6816 Valley View Road
Grebner, Hodne and Roberts, architects
1961 Honor Award

Modern Medicine Publications Building
(now Edina Realty)
4015 West 65th Street
Thorsen and Thorshov, architects
1963 Honorable Mention

Sturges Residence
6813 Oaklawn Avenue
Arthur Dickey, architect
1963 Honorable Mention

Braemar Golf Course Clubhouse
6364 Dewey Hill Road
Hammel, Green and Abrahamson, Inc., architects
1964 Merit Award

YMCA Southdale Branch
7355 York Avenue
Arthur Dickey Associates, architects
1975 Merit Award

Southdale-Hennepin Area Library
7001 York Avenue
Hodne/Stageberg Partnership, architects
1976 Merit Award

In 1980 the American Institute of Architects bestowed one of its national honor awards on the Colonial Church of Edina, 6200 Colonial Way, designed by Hammel, Green and Abrahamson, Inc.

Edina Realty, formerly Modern Medicine Publications, 4015 West 65th Street (above); St. Peter's Lutheran Church, 5421 France Avenue South (left).

Historic Building Sites Edina, Minnesota

① Baird House (1886)
4400 West 50th Street

② Blackbourn House (1939)
5015 Wooddale Lane

③ Cahill School (1864)
Frank Tupa Park at Eden Avenue and Highway 100

④ Calvary Lutheran Church (1938)
5420 West 70th Street

⑤ Carson House (1941)
6001 Pine Grove Road

⑥ Cornelius House (1910)
6101 France Avenue South

⑦ Dartt House (1910)
4500 West 44th Street

⑧ Dyer House (1913)
4379 Coolidge Avenue

⑨ Kimball House (1913)
4520 West 44th Street

⑩ Jalley House (1913)
4600 West 44th Street

⑪ Edina Baptist Church (1928)
5501 France Avenue South

⑫ Edina Theater (1934)
3911 West 50th Street

⑬ Erickson House (1911)
4246 Scott Terrace

⑭ Grange Hall (1879)
Frank Tupa Park at Eden Avenue and Highway 100

⑮ Grimes House (1869)
4200 West 44th Street

⑯ Leerskov House (1910)
4410 Curve Avenue

⑰ Morningside Congregational Church (1909, 1913)
4003 Morningside Road

⑱ Odd Fellows Hall (1918)
4388 France Avenue South

⑲ Onstad House (1915)
4305 Morningside Road

⑳ Peterson House (1880)
5312 Interlachen Boulevard

㉑ St. Patrick's Catholic Church (1924)
7000 Cahill Road

㉒ St. Stephen the Martyr Episcopal Church (1938)
West 50th Street at Wooddale Avenue

㉓ Simmons House (1911)
4116 West 44th Street

㉔ Skone House (1905-11)
4311 Eton Place

㉕ Sly House (1866-70)
6128 Brookview Avenue

㉖ Southdale Shopping Center (1954-56)
France Avenue South & West 66th Street

㉗ Trinity Chapel (1872)
4924 France Avenue South

㉘ Wooddale School (1926)
Wooddale Avenue and West 50th Street

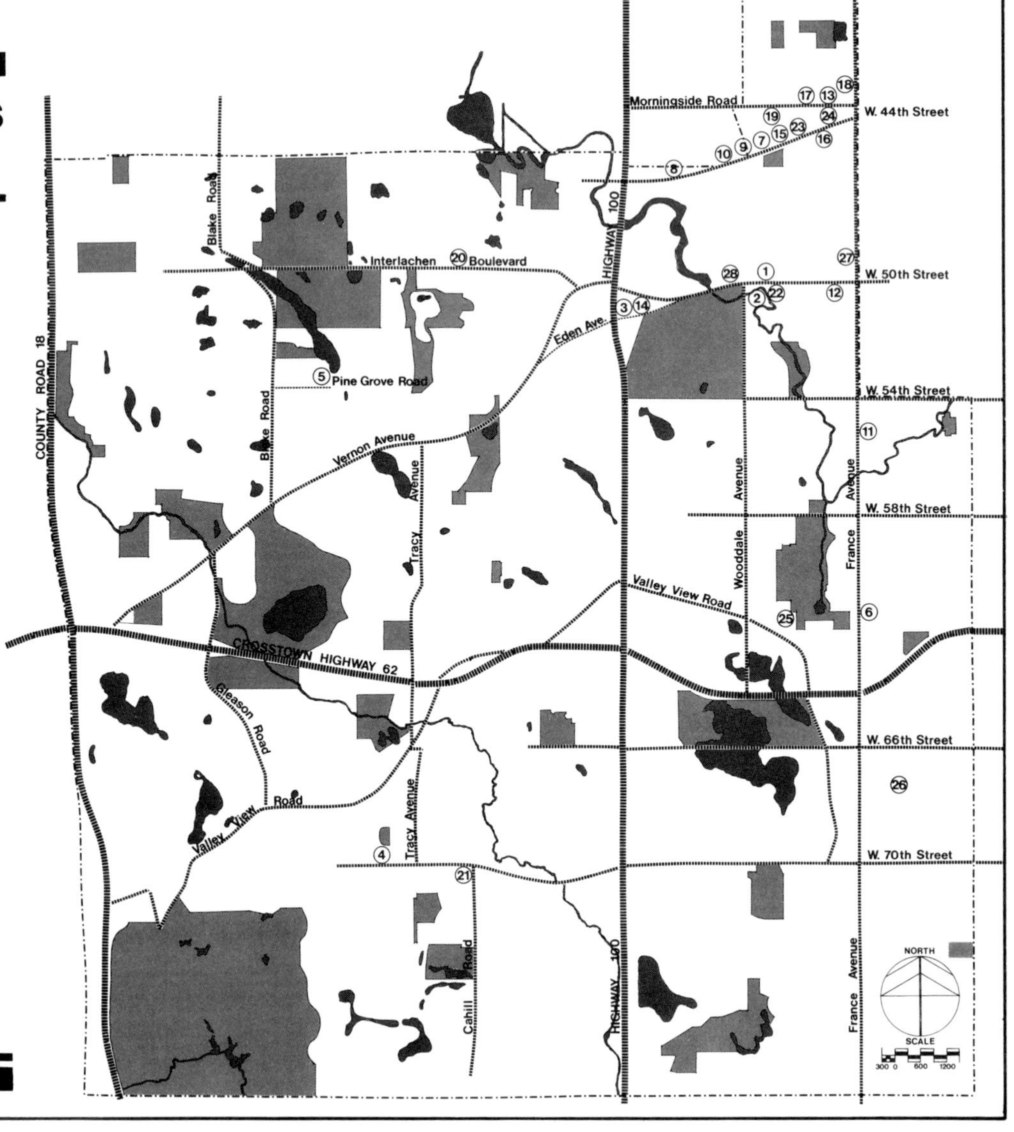

Site-Seeing: Significant Buildings and Districts

Edina is a city of over 12,000 buildings. In a very real sense, each of these structures is architecturally and historically significant. Each has an architectural style that reflects the circumstances of its construction. Each tells its own story of human occupancy and endeavor.

Yet architectural historians often insist that some buildings are indeed more significant than others. Such declarations should be treated with caution. It is well to ask, "Significant for whom?" The historian who is interested only in Gothic Revival buildings might conclude that the Grimes House is the only significant structure in Edina. Similarly, the student of nineteenth-century brownstone tenements might find nothing of architectural interest in the city at all. Statements of significance are never definitive judgments. They are merely judgments made from a particular perspective.

The perspective of this book is intentionally broad. Through intensive historical and architectural research, the authors have attempted to identify those buildings and districts in Edina that possess special significance for the general Edina public. Some of the sites selected have served the city's residents as major community centers. Familiar landmarks, they evoke the shared memories of a communal past. Other sites are increasingly rare examples of once popular architectural styles. To the knowing eye, they conjure up the mood and moment of a vanished era. Still other sites are the unique expression of gifted architectural design. They are works of art to be enjoyed by the entire community. Viewed as a whole, these special buildings and districts form a historic mosaic that gives Edina a character and identity different from all other cities.

1. Baird House
4400 West 50th Street
Charles S. Sedgwick, architect
1886

Baird House, 4400 West 50th Street, c. 1900 (above) and 1980 (opposite).

Immigrating to Minnesota from Pennsylvania in 1857, George W. Baird became one of the most prominent farmers in the Edina Mills community. Baird was an innovative livestock raiser who brought the first Merino sheep into the state. In 1880 his fine breeds of Cotswold and Lincoln sheep took first prizes at the Minneapolis Exposition.[1]

Always active in local politics, Baird by the early 1900s had become the patriarchal spokesman for those Edina residents who opposed the rapid suburbanization of their village. As Morningsider E. D. Parsons recalled in later years:

> [There was] "Old Man Baird" himself, rising after the subject of the meeting had been discussed for some time, and saying with great dignity, "Now, boys, I don't want you should think me unprogressive. I always want to see a good school and good roads and everything else to make us happy, but what I say is, go a little slow, boys."[2]

George W. Baird.

The mansion that Baird built for his family in 1886 reflected his station in the community. The building was unquestionably the most imposing residence in nineteenth-century Edina. Designed by Minneapolis architect Charles S. Sedgwick, the Baird House is a brick example of the Eastlake style. For visual interest, it depends primarily on a commanding square tower capped with a pyramidal roof. Other distinctive features include prominent chimneys, decorative shingle siding in the projecting attic gables, and stone trim at lintels, belt coursing, and windows.

Although remodeled on several occasions, the Baird House retains much of its original integrity. The principal exterior changes have involved replacement of the original wood-frame summer kitchen by an unobtrusive, one-story wing, removal of an attic dormer from the front of the house, and removal of scrollwork from the front porch.

Typical of the larger homes built in the late nineteenth century, the Baird House features a number of different woods in its interior design. The main stairway is white oak; the front parlor woodwork cherry; and the front entryway and dining-room wainscoting brown ash. Several original lighting fixtures and most of the original hardware and radiators remain. In recognition of its fine Victorian architecture, the Baird House has been placed on the National Register of Historic Places.

2. Blackbourn House
5015 Wooddale Lane
Royal Barry Wills, architect
1939

In an effort to stimulate new home construction and "pull the country out of the Depression," *Life* magazine in the summer of 1938 commissioned "the most distinguished architects in America" to design homes for "four representative American families" living in different parts of the country. The Albert R. Blackbourn family of Minneapolis was selected to represent the Midwest. The Blackbourns were given their choice of plans for a "traditional" home designed by Royal Barry Wills and a "modern" home designed by Frank Lloyd Wright. Both houses were in the $5,000 to $6,000 price range.[3] The Blackbourns chose Wills's design, explaining that Wright's "modern type home was a bit extreme, even for the twentieth century."[4]

Blackbourn House, 5015 Wooddale Lane.

Architect Royal Barry Wills of Boston, Massachusetts, was recognized as one of the outstanding practitioners of historic revival styles. He was known primarily for his Cape Cod cottages. Unlike the dry, stilted works of most of his contemporaries, Wills's buildings possessed a freshness and warmth that reflected the character of their seventeenth- and eighteenth-century predecessors. Long disdained by proponents of the modern school, his work is again receiving recognition.

The Blackbourn House is an example of Wills's Cape Cod cottage design. From the front, it appears as a low, one-story cottage with a large, wood-shingled roof dominated by a massive white brick chimney. Small, shuttered windows contain diamond-shaped panes. The front facade is white brick but the side and rear walls are white clapboard. A garage wing flanks the house. Seen from the street, the house looks deceptively small; because it is built on a sloping lot, the rear elevation consists of three levels.

Cahill School, Frank Tupa Park at Eden Avenue and Highway 100 (above). Children's artwork from Cahill School, c. 1910 (left).

3. Cahill School (School District No. 16) Frank Tupa Park at Eden Avenue and Highway 100 1864

Although lacking the traditional bell tower above the front entrance, Cahill School epitomizes in almost every other way the classic one-room schoolhouse of rural, nineteenth-century America. The building's general form and proportions, as well as its symmetrical placement of doors and windows, recall the Greek Revival style, which was still in vogue in Minnesota at the time of the school's construction in 1864.

Originally located on the southeast corner of Cahill Road and West 70th Street, Cahill School once stood at the geographic and spiritual center of the Irish Catholic community known as Cahill Settlement. Until 1884 the building was used as a chapel by the communicants of St. Patrick's Catholic Church. From 1933 to 1938 it served the same purpose for the congregation of Calvary Lutheran Church.[5]

In continuous classroom use until 1958, Cahill School was acquired by the Village of Edina in 1963 and moved to its present site in Frank Tupa Park. Under the auspices of the Edina Historical Society, which has its offices in the building's basement, the structure was restored and furnished to replicate its appearance in 1900. During the school year, costumed interpreters recreate the days of the one-room schoolhouse for children from Edina and neighboring communities. The oldest standing building in Edina, Cahill School is included in the National Register of Historic Places.[6]

4. Calvary Lutheran Church
5420 West 70th Street
1938

In 1933 a small group of Cahill area residents organized a branch of the Wooddale Lutheran Church to serve the needs of their immediate community. At first, services were held in the old Cahill School building, then located on the southeast corner of Cahill Road and West 70th Street. In 1936 the parishioners purchased a lot for $25 across the street from the school. Calvary Lutheran Church was erected on this site in the spring of 1938. "Measuring a scant 17 by 36 feet, its sanctuary had pew space for 60 worshipers and a choir."[7]

Within a decade the Calvary Lutheran congregation had outgrown its tiny chapel. In 1949 the church was enlarged with a concrete-block addition to the rear of the building.[8] Finally in 1960, the congregation constructed a new sanctuary at Antrim

Calvary Lutheran Church building, 5420 West 70th Street, c. 1960 (above) and 1980 (below).

Carson House, 6001 Pine Grove Road (above and below).

Road and West 69th Street. The old church was purchased by Rudolph E. Brom, a silversmith, who converted the building to a workshop-residence.[9]

Although the building has long served other purposes, its origins as a church are unmistakable. The design and character of this small, stucco-faced, frame structure are largely dependent upon its rectangular massing, its steep gable roofs over the nave and narthex, and its Gothic windows.

5. Carson House
6001 Pine Grove Road
William G. Purcell, architect
1941

On the exterior, this simple clapboard-sided, frame structure appears to have more in common with the Vernacular Farmhouse style than with the avant-garde Prairie School buildings for which its architect, William G. Purcell, is internationally acclaimed. On the interior, however, the building reveals the imaginative genius of its designer. Distinctive features include a large living room with a cathedral ceiling and a massive fireplace opening in the shape of a Gothic arch.

Paul and Mary Carson, who still reside in the house, commissioned the work in 1941 after a lengthy correspondence with their friend Purcell. The last residential design executed by Purcell, the Carson House is admirably sited in a park-like setting near Mirror Lake.[10]

6. Cornelius House
6101 France Avenue South
1910

When Adolph H. and Catherine Heiss Cornelius built this farmhouse in 1910, the surrounding countryside was mostly open farmland. Owning about thirty acres in the area, the Corneliuses were originally dairy farmers. During the 1920s they switched to truck farming, supplying Minneapolis wholesale merchants with fresh produce. Their daughter, Aldora Cornelius Hallaway, still resides in the house.[11]

The Cornelius House is an almost totally unaltered example of a "Midwest Square." As the description implies, the floor plan of this two-story, white clapboard-sided, frame structure is shaped like a square. The low hip roof culminates in a chimney. A single attic dormer faces the street. Wide eaves extend well beyond the exterior walls. The one-story front porch has been sympathetically enclosed. A well preserved example of a typical early-twentieth-century house, the building continues to serve efficiently and comfortably the purpose for which it was designed seventy years ago.

Cornelius House, 6101 France Avenue South.

Dartt House, 4500 West 44th Street.

This photograph of West 44th Street (c. 1910) appeared in one of George Dartt's promotional brochures for Browndale Park.

7. Dartt House
4500 West 44th Street
1910

One of the first houses in Browndale Park, this residence was erected and occupied by George and Alice Dartt in 1910. George Dartt, who owned a real estate and insurance business in Minneapolis, was an original promoter of the Browndale Park development.[12]

The Dartt House is a handsome and imaginative adaptation of Mission Revival architecture. The one-story, white stucco structure is dominated at one corner by an enclosed two-story tower with a low hip roof. All visible roof areas of the house are of red clay tile. An open porch projecting to the south and a similar, but enclosed, element to the west are covered with roofs hidden from view by high parapets with curvilinear gables. The large windows are somewhat more reminiscent of the Craftsman style than the Mission style. This fenestration, together with generous planting on the large corner lot, tends to soften the stark Mission effect. Consequently, the building does not look as out of place as most examples of this style in the Midwest.

8. Dyer House
4379 Coolidge Avenue
1913

9. Kimball House
4520 West 44th Street
1913

10. Jalley House
4600 West 44th Street
1913

Dyer House, 4379 Coolidge Avenue.

In 1905 the Twin City Rapid Transit Company inaugurated streetcar service between Minneapolis and Excelsior. The streetcar tracks traversed northeastern Edina along West 44th Street and stimulated a number of real estate ventures in the area. Browndale Park was perhaps the most fashionable of these early "streetcar suburbs." Platted in 1909 by Frank and Florence Mackey, the development lay mostly in St. Louis Park; its southern tip extended into Edina north of West 44th Street between Highway 100 and Wooddale Avenue.[13]

In certain respects, Browndale Park was a precursor of the Country Club District of the 1920s. Although Browndale Park was not as rigorously planned as Country Club, it maintained minimum set-back requirements and minimum building valuations ranging from $2,500 to $4,000.[14] The neighborhood provides some of Edina's earliest examples of historic revival architecture, which later became so popular in the Country Club District.

Kimball House, 4520 West 44th Street.

Jalley House, 4600 West 44th Street.

The residences at 4379 Coolidge Avenue, 4520 West 44th Street, and 4600 West 44th Street were built in 1913 by William C. Dyer, Claude D. Kimball, and William J. Jalley, respectively. Dyer and Kimball were Minneapolis businessmen; Jalley's occupation is unknown.[15] The three buildings, all located within a one-block radius, are the earliest known examples of English Tudor architecture in Edina. Given their proximity, identical date of construction, and similarity of style, the buildings may very well have been designed by the same architect to set a cohesive architectural standard for the neighborhood.

The Dyer and Kimball houses are especially faithful re-creations of their Elizabethan predecessors. Both have steep gable roofs, and second floors that project over the first floors. The Jalley House has a low-pitched gable roof reminiscent of the Craftsman style. Nevertheless, like its neighbors, the Jalley House exhibits such Tudor details as a brick veneer base below the first-floor windowsill line, and stucco infill between exposed half-timbering.

These three buildings constitute an important, well-coordinated collection of Tudor Revival houses. They represent a quality of design and construction that was not to be surpassed in later examples of the style built in the city.

11. Edina Baptist Church
5501 France Avenue South
1928

Originally known as the France Avenue Mission, this building was constructed in the summer of 1928 as a branch of the Lake Harriet Baptist Church. In 1942 the congregation established autonomy as the Edina Baptist Church. Six years later a new church building was completed at 5300 France Avenue South, and the former mission was converted into a private home.[16]

With the removal of the small steeple above the narthex wing, the church became an architecturally undistinguished residence. The clapboard facing of the one-story frame structure has been covered with blue composition siding up to the bottom of the eaves and with brown composition siding on the gable ends. There is a low, brown-shingled, gable roof over the main structure and entrance vestibule. The foundation is of concrete block. Although modest in architecture, the building is rich in historical significance.

Edina Baptist Church building, 5501 France Avenue South, c. 1945 (above) and 1980 (below).

Architectural drawing by Liebenberg and Kaplan for the Edina Theater (above); Edina Theater, 3911 West 50th Street (below).

12. Edina Theater
3911 West 50th Street
Liebenberg and Kaplan, architects
1934

The Country Club District remained a relatively stable community throughout the Depression. A sign of the district's general vitality was the construction of the nearby Edina Theater in 1934. The structure was designed to accommodate four retail shops, as well as a 1,300-seat motion picture theater equipped with "a public lounge, children's nursery, acoustical apparatus for hard of hearing, and air conditioning."[17]

With the recent demolition of the Edina Eye Clinic and the drastic alteration of the Westgate Theater, the Edina Theater is the only major example of the Art Deco style remaining in the city. Despite the replacement of the original canopy and entrance, and modifications to the building's "moderne" interior, a substantial amount of Liebenberg and Kaplan's original design remains. Unlike the Eye Clinic, which displayed soft round-cornered forms, the brick-faced theater exemplifies the hard-edged linear variation of Art Deco. The building's stepped, or ziggurat, tower is especially characteristic of the style.

13. Erickson House 4246 Scott Terrace 1911

This residence was built and occupied by Nels and Etta Erickson in 1911. Nels Erickson was manager of the Medium Hollow Block Machine Company in Minneapolis.[18]

The Alamo was conspicuously remembered in this outstanding, two-and-one-half-story example of a Mission Revival house. This architectural style, which enjoyed a brief popularity from about 1900 to 1915, was based on the Spanish-inspired buildings constructed by Indian labor in the American Southwest. From its rebirth in turn-of-the-century California, Mission Revival spread quickly throughout the country. The Erickson House authentically reflects its antecedants. Its walls are stark white and stuccoed. Its lintels are simple; and its porch columns and capitals are heavy, solid, and without ornament. Only the scalloped and parapeted gable ends with their round windows provide visual relief. The Erickson House is important as one of Minnesota's rare unaltered examples of Mission Revival architecture.

Erickson House, 4246 Scott Terrace.

Grange Hall, Frank Tupa Park at Eden Avenue and Highway 100 (above); interior of Grange Hall, date unknown (below).

14. Grange Hall (Minnehaha Grange No. 398)

Frank Tupa Park at Eden Avenue and Highway 100

1879

The Order of the Patrons of Husbandry, more commonly known as the Grange, was founded during the late 1860s by Oliver Hudson Kelley, a farmer from Sherburne County, Minnesota. According to Kelley's original plan, the Grange was to be a national "social fraternity of the farmers" dedicated to the principles of "progressive agriculture." "We want to bring in the whole farming community," wrote Kelley, ". . . set them to thinking that they are human beings, the strength of the nation, their labor honorable, and farming the highest calling on earth." By 1875 the Patrons of Husbandry had indeed become a national organization of farmers with thousands of chapters in over thirty states.[19]

Minnehaha Grange No. 398 was organized on December 12, 1873. Its members came primarily from Edina Mills, Richfield Mills, and the St. Louis Park area. In 1879 the Grangers built a meeting hall on the southeast corner of Wooddale Avenue and West 50th Street. In addition to its fraternal uses, this building also served as Edina Village Hall from 1888 to 1942.[20]

In 1935 the Grange Hall was moved from its original site to make way for the construction of St. Stephen the Martyr Episcopal Church. Relocated to the vicinity of Normandale Road and Eden Avenue, the hall was moved again in 1970 to its present site in Frank Tupa Park. As Edina farmyards gave way to suburban backyards, Minnehaha Grange evolved into a general social and fraternal order. Appropriately, the members of this oldest continuing Grange in Minnesota still conduct their meetings at the Grange Hall.[21]

In terms of its architecture, the Grange Hall is an early, rare Minnesota example of Stick style. Anticipating the later Craftsman and Prairie School movements, the proponents of this Victorian style attempted to strip away superfluous decoration in order to express the basic structural elements of the building. Ornamental "stickwork," which gives the style its name, was used to accentuate structural features. Typical Stick style details in the Grange Hall include vertical corner boards, simple hoods over windows, a slightly projecting bay supported by brackets, and decorative cross bracing in the gable end. Although this style conveys an almost skeletal austerity, the interplay of shadow and light on the stickwork adds a rich dimension to the design. For both its architectural and historical significance, the Grange Hall is listed in the National Register of Historic Places.

Jonathan T. Grimes.

15. Grimes House
4200 West 44th Street
1869

The inhabitants of Morningside in the early 1900s saw themselves as hardy pioneers bringing residential order to undeveloped countryside. But this section of northeastern Edina was undeveloped only in an urban sense. From an agricultural stand-

This illustration of the Grimes House from the 1870s appeared on Jonathan T. Grimes's personal stationery.

Grimes House, 4200 West 44th Street.

point, the land had been under cultivation for almost half a century. The first permanent settler in the area was Jonathan T. Grimes, a transplanted Virginian who purchased Waterville Mills (later known as Edina Mills) and 160 acres of adjoining land in 1859. Grimes operated the mill for ten years and then turned exclusively to farming.[22]

The first president of the Minnesota Horticultural Society, Grimes had a reputation for agricultural experimentation. Devoting part of his homestead to a commercial apple orchard and tree nursery, he grew the first Gingko and catalpa trees in the state. His nursery also supplied the shade trees that still border Hennepin, Lyndale, and University avenues in Minneapolis.[23]

In 1869 Grimes built a clapboard-sided, frame dwelling that is now one of Edina's oldest and most charming residences. One and one-half stories in height, the Grimes House sympathetically combines two major architectural styles. The sharply sloping roofs and pointed-arch windows in the gable ends bear the signature of Gothic Revival, while the bracketed, wide, overhanging eaves and first-floor projecting bay are unmistakably Italianate. At the turn of the century, the original kitchen at the rear of the building was replaced by the present two-story wing. At the same time, several interior partitions were removed, and a fireplace was installed in the dining room.

The Grimes House is currently undergoing extensive restoration to bring the building closer to its original appearance. The structure is listed in the National Register of Historic Places as a rare, surviving example of the Gothic Revival style in the Twin Cities area.

16. Leerskov House 4410 Curve Avenue c. 1910

Niels N. Leerskov was a prominent builder in the Morningside area. He erected this house as his family residence about 1910. The first Morningside settler to be elected to the Edina Village Council, Leerskov spearheaded the secession of Morningside from Edina in 1920. He served as the first treasurer of the Village of Morningside.[24]

This large, two-and-one-half-story, clapboard-sided, frame residence is a product of its period. It combines in one structure the characteristics of several popular architectural styles. In plan, it is a Midwest Square. In the four equal-sized gables, there are Colonial Revival Palladian windows. The distinct separation between the stucco-faced first floor and the wood siding above is characteristic of Craftsman houses; the shallow, projecting bays are elements commonly used in both Craftsman and Bungalow houses. The Leerskov House merits recognition as a well preserved expression of the architectural tastes of prosperous middle America at the beginning of the twentieth century.

Leerskov House, 4410 Curve Avenue.

Morningside Congregational Church building, 4003 Morningside Road, c. 1910 (above) and 1980 (below).

17. Morningside Congregational Church 4003 Morningside Road E. H. Lund, architect 1909, 1913

One of the first settlers in newly platted Morningside was Henry W. Parsons, a retired Congregational minister. With his neighbors' encouragement, Parsons helped found the Morningside Congregational Church. The first chapel, erected at 4003 Morningside Road in 1909, was modest in the extreme. Contemporary accounts refer to it as a "little box-like structure, looking like a birdhouse magnified."[25] By 1913 the parishioners had raised $4,500 to enlarge and remodel the building. Architectural plans were prepared by E. H. Lund; they called for "an auditorium to seat 125 persons, a Sunday school room with nearly that capacity . . . a modern kitchen and a . . . shower bath in case gymnastics are attempted in the future."[26] The remodeled building continued to serve as a chapel until the congregation moved to larger quarters in the early 1920s. It is now a private residence.

Today this modest stucco-faced cottage, with its modified Tudor chimney and suggestion of half-timbering, gives little indication that it was once a church. The most distinctive feature of the present building is its steep jerkinhead roof, formed when the church's original gable roof was sliced off at the top. An enclosed front porch replaces the original narthex. In its materials, scale, and character, the building blends well into a neighborhood filled with one-story and one-and-one-half-story Bungalow, Craftsman, and Mission Revival houses.

18. Odd Fellows Hall
4388 France Avenue South
1918

In 1918, Golden Link Lodge No. 167 constructed a two-story brick building at the corner of France Avenue South and West 44th Street to serve as a fraternal meeting hall. The retail spaces on the ground floor were originally occupied by a restaurant and a dry goods store.[27] The Odd Fellows Hall became a social center for the Morningside community. Morningside resident and historian E. D. Parsons has described the building's early importance:

> Not only are lodge meetings and social functions held there, but regular Saturday afternoon dancing classes, neighborhood parties and entertainments, and the services of the Morningside [Congregational] Church and Sunday School. The hall is equipped with kitchen accommodations and has a stage for amateur dramatic performances. There is a commodious reception room and there are two other rooms available. The hall is occupied nearly every night of the week.[28]

There are few pretentions to architectural style in this utilitarian building. Its principal section is a two-story rectangle topped with a low hip roof. The one-story wing attached to the north side has a flat roof. Because the Odd Fellows Hall has played an integral role in the commercial, social, civic, and religious life of Morningside, it deserves preservation as one of the city's significant historic structures.

Odd Fellows Hall, 4388 France Avenue South.

Onstad House, 4305 Morningside Road.

Peterson House, 5312 Interlachen Boulevard.

19. Onstad House 4305 Morningside Road c. 1915

This residence was apparently constructed about 1915 for Henry and Lois Onstad by Niels Leerskov, a prominent building contractor in the Morningside area. Shortly after the dwelling's completion, Onstad was elected president of the Edina Village Council.[29]

The Onstad House is a fine example of the California Bungalow style, adapted to a northern climate and setting. Its distinctive features include horizontal wood siding that extends from grade level to the first-floor window heads, a banded pattern of fenestration, and low-pitched roofs with deep overhangs braced by heavy strut supports. As a result of its strong horizontal lines, the building appears almost to hug the ground. The feeling of intimacy is further heightened by a lack of symmetry in the facades and by an informal floor plan. A large brick chimney dominates the whole ensemble.

20. Peterson House 5312 Interlachen Boulevard c. 1880

Paul Peterson built and occupied this residence about 1880. He retained ownership of the property for at least the next forty years.[30]

No other building in Edina contains the amount of late-Victorian "gingerbread" exhibited by this Eastlake-style residence. The turned spindles, jigsaw work, and decorative shingles in the gable end, as well as the angular trim surrounding the tall, narrow second-story window, are architectural details seldom seen in the city. Only the later addition of an enclosed porch and double-hung windows detract from the overall effect. Well maintained and handsomely restored, the Peterson House is architecturally significant as one of Edina's few frame houses in the Eastlake style.

21. St. Patrick's Catholic Church 7000 Cahill Road 1924

During the 1850s and 1860s, southern Edina was settled primarily by Irish immigrants, who named their community "Cahill." The center of the Cahill Settlement was the junction of Cahill Road and West 70th Street. At the southeast corner of this intersection, the settlers erected in 1864 the Cahill School, which also served as a meeting place for St. Patrick's Catholic Church.[31] Twenty years later a separate church building was constructed at the southwest corner of the intersection. When this small, steepled church was destroyed by lightning in 1924, the present structure was immediately built on the same site.[32] This building continued to serve as a church until November 1961, when the congregation moved to a newly completed sanctuary at 6779 Valley View Road.[33]

The old church is a utilitarian, one-story rectangular structure set on a high base of molded concrete block. The most distinctive feature of the building is its decorative half-timbering. A band of horizontal clapboard siding resembling a wainscot

St. Patrick's Catholic Church building, 7000 Cahill Road.

Architect Louis B. Bersback's drawing of St. Stephen the Martyr Episcopal Church (above); the church at West 50th Street and Wooddale Avenue (below).

extends from the top of the foundation wall to the windowsills. Walls above that band are white-painted stucco. Important for its historical associations, the building perpetuates the memory of Cahill Settlement.

22. St. Stephen the Martyr Episcopal Church

West 50th Street and Wooddale Avenue

Louis B. Bersback, and Cram and Ferguson, architects

1938

Inspired by the parish churches of rural England, this Gothic Revival structure of rough and dressed limestone is handsomely sited on grounds adjoining Minnehaha Creek. The building was designed by Louis B. Bersback in consultation with the architectural firm of Cram and Ferguson, which was nationally known for its interpretations of late Gothic Revival buildings.[34] Noteworthy details include the large west window with its Flamboyant Gothic stone tracery, and the charming wooden porch reminiscent of those in the timber districts of Britain. Although massive in its proportions, the building achieves a picturesque quality through its long nave, compact crenellated tower, and well designed details. Despite extensive additions, St. Stephen's remains a faithful interpretation of an English country church.

23. Simmons House 4116 West 44th Street 1911

In 1910 William and Lillian Riley purchased several lots on West 44th Street in the recently platted "Grimes Homestead" section of Morningside. The Rileys were real estate speculators, and they replatted their property into several small parcels.[35] In an apparent attempt to give "tone" to their venture, they established deed restrictions that were more typical of fashionable Browndale Park than of the Morningside area. When Alfred and Jessie Simmons purchased a lot from the Rileys, they were required to erect "a new modern residence, costing not less than $2,500, and containing not less than six rooms of the average size . . . set back at least 35 feet from the front line. . . ."[36]

The Simmonses patterned their home after a Bungalow they had seen during a trip to California. Alfred Simmons, a Minneapolis millwright, may have drawn up the plans himself.[37] The building is undoubtedly one of the city's most handsome residences. Typical of Craftsman Bungalows, the house has strong, low horizontal lines. It exhibits great sensitivity in the massing of the low-pitched gable roofs and pergola, and in the interplay of building forms and materials. The total effect is almost Japanese in character.

Simmons House, 4116 West 44th Street, c. 1911 (above) and 1980 (below).

Skone House, 4311 Eton Place.

24. Skone House
4311 Eton Place
c. 1905-11

All of the lots in the original plat of Morningside measured at least 100 by 200 feet, providing early residents with sufficient space to indulge in some of the joys of rural living. Stables, chicken coops, and garden plots were common accoutrements of the early Morningside home.[38] But as Morningside real estate appreciated in value, many residents were willing to sacrifice pastoral charm for profit; they constructed additional houses on their property for sale or rental to newly arrived city folk.

Oliver and Iva Skone were among the early Morningside residents who turned builders. In 1905 the Skones purchased a large lot fronting the entire east side of Eton Place. During the next six years, they erected three houses at 4307, 4311, and 4313 Eton Place.[39] Iva supervised the construction activities, while Oliver worked in Minneapolis as a printer. The Skones occupied one of the houses as a residence and apparently managed the other two as rental properties.[40]

This house is one of the area's smallest and most delightful examples of Mission Revival architecture, a California-inspired style based on early Spanish and American Indian building designs. Characteristics of the style are the Skone House's plain, white stucco walls and small window openings topped by pronounced curvilinear gables.

25. Sly House
6128 Brookview Avenue
1866-70

Parts of this farmhouse may date from as early as 1866, when Gilbert and Mary Sly and their children took possession of a 160-acre homestead in the area. Before settling in Minnesota, the Slys had been farmers in New York State. Their oldest daughter Fidelia retained ownership of the farmhouse until 1901.[41]

Although this one-and-one-half-story, clapboard-sided, frame building has undergone many alterations, it retains a quality of rural remoteness in an otherwise thoroughly suburban neighborhood. Built on a hilltop, it sits askew from the street which it now fronts. The original foundations are stone, while those of more recent additions are concrete. Despite such later additions as an attached garage, dormer windows, oversized fenestration in the front facade, a large white brick chimney, and vertical board-and-batten siding on the porch, the building still manages to convey a sense of its pre-1870 origin. The Sly House is significant as one of the city's few remaining farmhouses with site and structure sufficiently intact to evoke a mood of pre-suburban Edina.

Sly House, 6128 Brookview Avenue.

Southdale Shopping Center, France Avenue South and West 66th Street.

26. Southdale Shopping Center

France Avenue South and West 66th Street

Victor Gruen and Associates, architects

1954-56

In April 1929, Edina became the first village in Minnesota to adopt a comprehensive zoning ordinance.[42] Twenty-five years later, it enhanced its reputation as a well planned community by approving the construction of the Southdale Shopping Center. Southdale not only provides Edina residents with premier shopping facilities, but also significantly strengthens and diversifies the city's tax base.

Designed by Victor Gruen and Associates, Southdale was the nation's first enclosed, regional shopping center. A model for similar facilities throughout the country, Southdale revolutionized American retailing methods and shopping habits. Its opening in 1955 was a major architectural event described in detail by *Architectural Forum:*

> The Southdale environment is quite unlike that of any other shopping center. There is nothing suburban about it except its location. For Southdale uncannily conveys the feeling of a metropolitan downtown: the magical, intangible assurance that here is the big time, this is where things happen, here is the middle of things. Consider that this is done in what is just a single building and without any of downtown's entertainment world to help and it becomes even more astounding.[43]

As originally designed, the vast complex was defined by two, two-story masses located at opposite ends of the building. Each of these dominant forms contained a major department store. Linking these elements were a series of smaller, block-shaped retail spaces that clustered around an enclosed court rising two stories in height. The court was lighted by a clerestory and skylight, as well as by auxiliary, artificial illumination. Convenient customer access to both levels was provided on the outside by bilevel parking lots and on the inside by conspicuously located escalators and stairways.

When first opened, Southdale occupied a site of eighty-four acres. To ensure that adjacent development would be compatible with the center, an additional 400 acres surrounding the site were acquired. This area is now occupied by office, apartment, medical, and commercial facilities.

27. Trinity Chapel
4924 France Avenue South
1872

The oldest church building still standing in Edina, Trinity Chapel was erected as an Episcopalian mission in 1872. It was officially known as the Chapel of Brotherhood of Gethsemane Trinity, Oak Grove. According to diocesan records, the new chapel was well appointed, "being carpeted, having stained glass windows, . . . and provided with a font, surplice, organ, etc. . . ."[44] During the late 1880s, the chapel was converted into a private dwelling. Originally located on the northwest corner of France Avenue South and West 50th Street, it was moved to its present site in 1925 to make room for a commercial

Trinity Chapel building, 4924 France Avenue South.

Wooddale School, Wooddale Avenue and West 50th Street.

block.[45] The building is now occupied by an interior decorating studio.

In its original form, Trinity Chapel was a one-story, frame building surmounted by a bell steeple.[46] Its present configuration strongly suggests the Greek Revival style, particularly in its form, proportions, and gable-end returns at the eaves. However, the window and door openings in the east (France Avenue) elevation are atypical of construction methods and design for both the original construction date and the 1880s remodeling. It is believed that these openings represent revisions made during later building remodeling programs. The glass-enclosed, gable-roofed entrance portico recently replaced an open, shed-roofed portico of undetermined vintage. The concrete foundation walls date from the time of the building's relocation in 1925.

28. Wooddale School
Wooddale Avenue & West 50th Street
Sund and Dunham, architects
1926

Although Morningside seceded from Edina and became a separate village in 1920, it remained part of Edina Independent School District No. 17. The schoolhouse serving this district was a small brick structure located on the present site of Edina City Hall. Erected in the late 1880s for a farming community, the building was clearly inadequate for a burgeoning suburban population.[47]

By 1920 both villages recognized the need for a new school building, but they could not agree on its location. The residents of Edina wished to keep the new schoolhouse on the old site; the residents of Morningside wanted a location closer to their village. Between 1920 and 1924, eleven referendums failed to resolve the deadlock. Finally in November 1925, the two villages compromised by agreeing to build a new schoolhouse in each community. The next year saw the completion of both buildings: Morningside School at Grimes Avenue and West 42nd Street, and Wooddale School at Wooddale Avenue and West 50th Street.

Morningside School fell victim to demolition in 1979. Retired from active classroom use in 1980, Wooddale School may eventually find a similar fate. With its high ceilings, brick face, and flat roof, the building typifies the schoolhouses of the 1920s and 1930s. Its original plan called for "a two-story and basement structure, containing 12 classrooms, gymnasium, auditorium for 1,100 people, lunchroom, offices, restrooms, and a library." The building was substantially enlarged by a rear addition in 1936.[48]

Ornamental relief on Wooddale School is provided by details in the Spanish Colonial Revival style, concentrated mainly around the doorways. The main entrance is recessed behind a stone-arch arcade supported by stone columns. Above is a curvilinear parapet centered over the second-story windows. The windows are set in a panel embellished with twisted columns, finials, and a broken pediment. An important architectural and historical adjunct of the Country Club District, Wooddale School merits continued preservation.

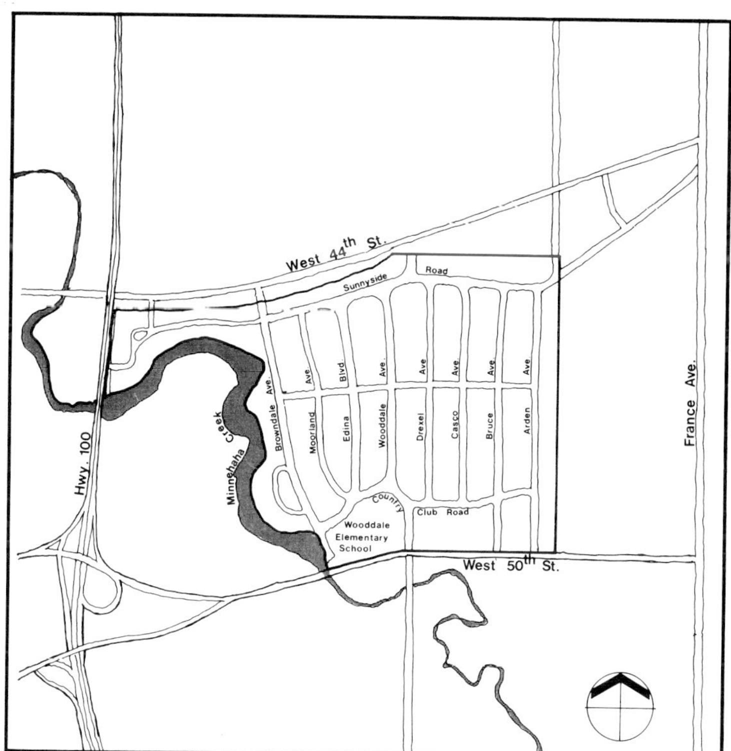

Country Club District Brown and Fairway Sections

Today Edina is recognized as an exclusive suburban community. This image is of long standing. It dates back over half a century to the founding of the Country Club District by Samuel Thorpe of Thorpe Bros. In 1922 Thorpe purchased the Browndale Farm from the H. F. Brown estate. On this site, once the heart of the old Edina Mills community, Thorpe planned to develop "one of the finest residence districts" in the country.[49]

Unlike previous real estate developers, such as the Grimes family in Morningside and Tingdale Brothers in Brookside, Thorpe was not interested in merely platting a district and selling lots. Instead he envisioned a thoroughly planned community governed by "wise but rigid building restrictions." Modeling his venture after J. C. Nichols's Country Club District in Kansas City, Missouri, Thorpe landscaped his development with contoured streets, parks, and an eighteen-hole golf course. He also installed major utility services, including water, gas, electricity, and sewers. "Property owners," he announced, "will not have their yards disfigured with digging of cesspools nor their streets mutilated by the laying of sewage or water mains. This has all been taken care of in advance . . . ."[50]

After spending two years and over $1,000,000 in designing his development, Thorpe in the spring of 1924 formally submitted two adjoining plats of the Country Club District to the Edina Village Council. According to these plats, the original boundaries of the district were the streetcar tracks along West 44th

Country Club District, c. 1930.

ALONG THE CREEK

CREEKS and lakes are nature's choicest gifts to the artistry of her landscapes. Minnesota is generously endowed with these sparkling adornments. Circumstances, however, do not always permit the rarest beauty spots to become the nucleus for a metropolitan home district. The Country Club District is most fortunate in this respect. Minnehaha Creek, within the boundaries of the Country Club District is really a lake or series of lakes. Lake Minnetonka, which is the source of Minnehaha Creek, furnishes the supply of fresh water; the dam at Fiftieth Street fixes the level of the lake, which is within the confines of the Country Club District.

Page from a promotional brochure for the Country Club District.

Street on the north, Arden Avenue on the east, West 50th Street and Minnehaha Creek on the south, and Normandale Road on the west.[51]

The plats divided Country Club into two sections: Brown Section to the west of Wooddale Avenue, and Fairway Section to the east. The primary distinction between the two sections concerned restrictions in minimum building valuations. The least expensive building permitted in Brown Section was $7,500; in Fairway Section, $6,000.[52] Otherwise the two sections shared essentially the same restrictions, which are, in part, listed below:

> All lots [with a few specified exceptions] . . . are hereby designated "residence lots" and shall not be improved, used or occupied for other than private one-family residence purposes; . . . there shall not be erected . . . on any of said lots any flats, duplexes, apartments, . . . public garages, oil stations or any other buildings whatsoever except a detached dwelling house to be used exclusively as a residence for a single family (with out-buildings to be used exclusively for domestic purposes) of not less than 1-1/2 stories in height . . . with a cellar . . . .
>
> No residence, or other structure, shall, prior to July 1, 1944, be erected or maintained on any lot until the plans, specifications, elevation, location and grade thereof, with color scheme for said residence or structure, shall first have been presented to the vendor and approved in writing . . . .
>
> All out-buildings shall correspond in style and architecture to the residence to which such buildings are appurtenant . . . .
>
> No tank for the storage of fuel shall be maintained above the surface of the ground.
>
> No sign greater than 480 square inches shall be placed on any lot, except those of the vendor.

No shedding poplars, box elders or other objectionable trees or shrubbery shall be planted.

No garbage, ashes, refuse or refuse receptacles shall be placed or left on any lot so as to be exposed to view, or become a nuisance.

No horses, cows, goats, sheep or any domestic animals, poultry or fowls of any kind, except dogs and cats, will be permitted to be kept on any of the lots, except a riding horse or horses with the written consent of the vendor.

No soft coal, except smokeless coal, nor fuel of any kind giving off black smoke, or strong or obnoxious odors, shall be used.

No lot shall ever be sold, conveyed, leased or rented to any person other than of the white or Caucasian race, nor shall any lot ever be used or occupied by any person other than of the white or Caucasian race, except such as may be serving as domestics for the owner or tenant of said lot, while said owner or tenant is residing thereon.[53]

As Thorpe's promotional brochure carefully pointed out, these building restrictions were designed to make Country Club a community of "the exclusive and select" — "a community where you can be proud to live, proud of your home . . . and of your neighbor's home as well."[54] Despite the district's unique qualities, it was slow to attract residents. According to Thorpe's son, Samuel Thorpe, Jr., "it took a while to sell . . . the idea of moving such a long way from established Minneapolis neighborhoods."[55] To stimulate interest in his development, Thorpe in 1926 commissioned the Minneapolis architectural firm of Liebenberg and Kaplan to design at least seven model homes in a variety of

Cutting hay on empty lots in the Country Club District, 1932.

Model homes designed by Liebenberg and Kaplan: 4612 Moorland Avenue (above) and 4617 Moorland Avenue (below).

historic revival styles. Ranging from English Tudor to French Provincial to American Colonial, these residences were completed in 1927. Five of the model homes have been identified at the following addresses: 4608, 4614, and 4619 Edina Boulevard; and 4612 and 4617 Moorland Avenue.[56] To a considerable degree, the Liebenberg and Kaplan designs set an architectural standard for later construction in the district.

Thorpe's continual promotional efforts eventually succeeded. By 1930 the Country Club District contained 269 houses and over 1,000 residents — nearly one-third of Edina's total population. Although construction slowed during the early years of the Depression, it surged ahead with the upturn in the economy after 1936.[57] A demographic analysis of the 1930 *Country Club Directory* reveals the basic profile of an upper-middle-class community: 591 adults, 344 minors, and 97 servants. Of approximately 150 men in the district on whom data has been collected, 26 worked in wholesale or retail merchandising, 25 in real estate or insurance, 26 in the professions, 14 in finance, and 28 in various self-employed businesses.[58]

The architecture of the Country Club District mirrors the tastes of the prosperous executive and professional classes of the 1920s-1940s. Of the approximately 550 residences in the neighborhood, a total of 97 percent are inspired by historic revival styles. The most popular designs are American Colonial (38 percent), English Tudor (24 percent), English Cottage (13 percent), and Mediterranean (13 percent).[59] Although several of the buildings are the work of such architects as A. R. Van Dyck, C. W. Farnham, Milton C. W. Sundim, Carl J. Bard, and

J. V. Vanderbilt, the majority of the dwellings were evidently designed and built by contractors. Carl Hansen, Louis Hanson, and Anton Duoos were especially prominent builders in the area.[60] Viewed separately, few of the buildings in Country Club are architecturally unique. But the district as a whole has a rare cohesiveness. As architectural historians David Gebhard and Tom Martinson have observed, "the houses . . . established a strong sense of place which is not often found in American cities."[61]

During its early years, the Country Club District formed a self-conscious and virtually self-contained community, easily distinguishable from other Edina residential areas by its affluence, architecture, and landscaping. During the late 1930s, however, the original Brown and Fairway sections were gradually surrounded by newly platted residential districts of similar economic status.[62] The architectural boundaries of Country Club slowly dissolved into a larger suburban streetscape. By 1939 the *Country Club Directory* had changed its name to the *Directory of Metropolitan Edina*.[63]

The architectural and historical significance of Thorpe's Country Club District is manifold. On a national level, it is one of the handful of "high-class" residential developments built in the 1920s on the pattern of Nichols's Kansas City Country Club.[64] On a municipal level, it marks the transformation of a predominantly rural community into a major metropolitan suburb dedicated to the principles of city planning. In many respects, modern Edina had its beginnings in Thorpe's decision to create a residential suburb "superior in every sense of the word to any sub-division or residential property ever before put on the market in this part of the country."[65]

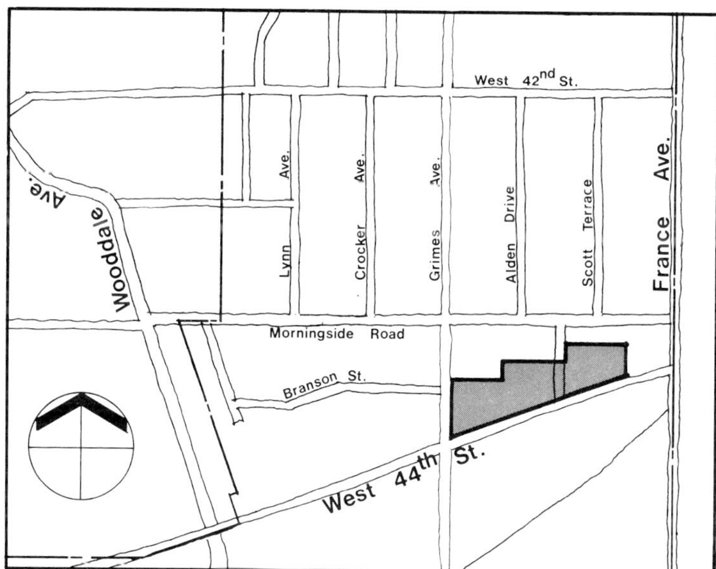

A typical residence in the Morningside Bungalow District: 4006 West 44th Street.

Morningside Bungalow District North Side of West 44th Street between France Avenue South and Grimes Avenue

The area of northeastern Edina bounded roughly by Wooddale Avenue, West 40th Street, France Avenue South, and West 44th Street is commonly known as Morningside. For almost half a century, this area comprised the smallest village in Minnesota. Morningside seceded from Edina in 1920 and rejoined its parent community in 1966.

At the beginning of the twentieth century, the region was open farmland owned primarily by the Grimes family. When the Twin City Rapid Transit Company in 1905 announced plans to extend streetcar service to the area, Morningside was quickly platted and settled.[66] Early residents were mostly white-collar workers who commuted to their jobs in Minneapolis. By 1920, Morningside contained about 500 of Edina's 1,833 people.[67]

The architecture of early Morningside reflected the modest circumstances of the community's inhabitants. Of the approximately 100 surviving houses of pre-1920 construction, almost half are Bungalow-type structures.[68] The Bungalow style emphasized inexpensive, easily maintained materials, such as stucco, wood siding, brick, field stone, and stock millwork; an exposed structural system unencumbered by decorative moldings; and an informal, efficient floor plan. For all these reasons, it was especially appealing to middle-income families.

Although Bungalows are found scattered throughout Morningside, a particularly choice collection is located on the north side of West 44th Street between France Avenue South and Grimes Avenue. The residences in this two-block area aptly demonstrate the diversity of materials and design of the Bungalow style in Morningside. Noteworthy examples are the dwellings at 3920, 4006, 4010, 4012, 4014, 4016, 4018, and 4020 West 44th Street (c. 1910 - c. 1920). A showcase of early Morningside's most popular architectural style, this area merits recognition as a historic municipal district.

West Minneapolis Heights District East Side of Jefferson Avenue between South Third Street and Belmore Lane; Madison Avenue between South Third Street and Belmore Lane

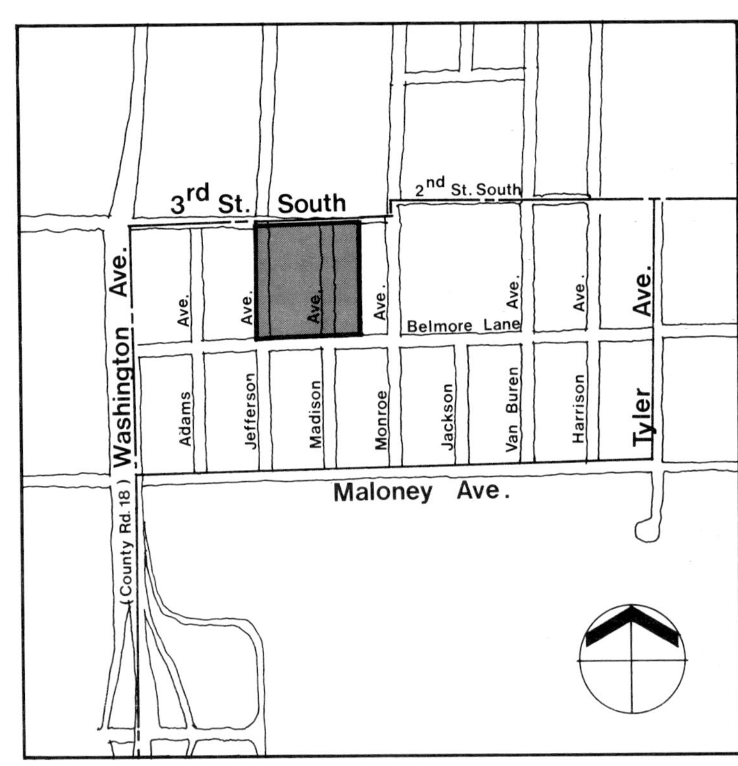

In 1887 the Minneapolis Threshing Machine Company (later known as Minneapolis-Moline) established a manufacturing plant in West Minneapolis (later known as Hopkins). Providing employment for several hundred people, the factory became the center of a blue-collar residential neighborhood that extended into the extreme northwest corner of Edina. This section of Edina was platted in 1887 as West Minneapolis Heights by Charles P. Silloway, a Minneapolis real estate broker.[69]

West Minneapolis Heights is bounded by Tyler Avenue on the east, Maloney Avenue on the south, and Hopkins on the west and north. From the outset, Silloway apparently intended the community to be a residential adjunct of the Hopkins industrial district. His plans, however, were cut short by the Depression of 1893. The Minneapolis Threshing Machine Company reduced its operations, and Silloway lost much of his property through foreclosures. Before the crash, Silloway seems to have erected seven dwellings in the district. It is unclear whether these structures were built for immediate sale or for rental. Four of these buildings appear to survive on their original sites at 315 and 319 Madison Avenue and 401 and 403 Washington Avenue.[70]

Two residences in the West Minneapolis Heights District: 403 Washington Avenue (above) and 308 Madison Avenue (below).

After the collapse of Silloway's real estate venture, West Minneapolis Heights remained dormant for over a decade. The improvement in general economic conditions after 1900 gradually brought renewed residential construction to the area. Surviving buildings dating from 1900 to 1920 include residences at 303, 305, 307, 308, 312, 313, and 316 Madison Avenue; and 305, 307, 309, 313, and 317 Jefferson Avenue.

West Minneapolis Heights provides an architectural vista unique in Edina. The Midwest Square, Midwest Saltbox, and Vernacular Farmhouse residences on Madison and Jefferson avenues conjure up an image of small-town Minnesota at the turn of the century. Buildings of similar design and age are found elsewhere in Edina, but only in West Minneapolis Heights do they appear in sufficient density to form an extended streetscape. Although some of the structures have additions and many have lost their original clapboard siding, most of the buildings retain stylistic authenticity.

Inventory of Surviving Structures Erected Before 1900

The following list was compiled on the basis of documentary research, interviews with past and present Edina residents, and field inspections of the city's standing structures. Dates are supplied only when they have been substantiated by reliable documentary sources. Asterisks denote conflicting evidence concerning a structure's pre-1900 status. Future research may justify additions and/or deletions. Unless otherwise noted, all of these buildings were originally designed as private residences.

6501 Belmore Lane
5717 Blake Road (1878)
6128 Brookview Avenue (1866-70)
5 Cooper Avenue
*4428 Dunberry Lane
Eden Avenue and Highway 100; Cahill School (1864)
Eden Avenue and Highway 100; Grange Hall (1879)
6125 Ewing Avenue
4924 France Avenue South; Trinity Chapel (1872)
408 Griffit Street
5312 Interlachen Boulevard (c. 1880)
5419 Interlachen Boulevard
5801 Interlachen Boulevard
315 Madison Avenue (c. 1893)
319 Madison Avenue (c. 1893)
4835 Valley View Road
*6932 Valley View Road
401 Washington Avenue (c. 1893)
403 Washington Avenue (c. 1893)
6220 Waterman Avenue
6309 Waterman Avenue
4200 44th Street West (1869)
*5125 49th Street West
4400 50th Street West (1886)
4812 70th Street West
5524 70th Street West

Inventory of Surviving Structures Erected 1900-1920

The following list was compiled primarily on the basis of research in Edina Assessor's Office files and field inspections of the city's standing structures. Future research may justify additions and/or deletions. Unless otherwise noted, all of these buildings were originally designed as private residences.

6009 Abbott Avenue
4220 Alden Drive
4223 Alden Drive
4224 Alden Drive
4226 Alden Drive
4227 Alden Drive
4230 Alden Drive
4237 Alden Drive
4240 Alden Drive
4243 Alden Drive
4244 Alden Drive
4246 Alden Drive
4248 Alden Drive
308 Arthur Street
5913 Ashcroft Avenue
5929 Ashcroft Avenue

6233 Belmore Lane
6509 Belmore Lane
6615 Belmore Lane
5512 Benton Avenue
306 Blake Road
420 Blake Road
604 Blake Road
5201 Blake Road
5309 Blake Road
4206 Branson Street
4208 Branson Street
4209 Branson Street
4210 Branson Street
4212 Branson Street
4300 Branson Street
4304 Branson Street
4306 Branson Street
4308 Branson Street
4314 Branson Street
4315 Branson Street
4401 Branson Street

4351 Brookside Avenue
4355 Brookside Avenue
4412 Brookside Avenue
4512 Brookside Avenue
4528 Brookside Avenue
4532 Brookside Avenue
4810 Brookside Avenue
5243 Brookside Court
4433 Brookside Terrace
4437 Brookside Terrace
4517 Brookside Terrace
6129 Brookview Avenue
6143 Brookview Avenue
6144 Brookview Avenue

7100 Cahill Road
7440 Cahill Road
4379 Coolidge Avenue
4243 Crocker Avenue
4244 Crocker Avenue
4245 Crocker Avenue
4246 Crocker Avenue
4409 Curve Avenue
4410 Curve Avenue
5216 Division Street
5217 Division Street
4303 Eton Place
4304 Eton Place
4307 Eton Place
4311 Eton Place
4313 Eton Place
4316 Eton Place
6129 Ewing Avenue

4224 France Avenue South
4228 France Avenue South
4232 France Avenue South
4238 France Avenue South
4242 France Avenue South
4250 France Avenue South
4300 France Avenue South
4308 France Avenue South
4312 France Avenue South
4320 France Avenue South
4330 France Avenue South
4350 France Avenue South
4352 France Avenue South
4388 France Avenue South (Odd Fellows Hall)
5102 France Avenue South
5120 France Avenue South
5208 France Avenue South
5440 France Avenue South
6101 France Avenue South
6204 France Avenue South
3704 Fuller Street

6328 Gleason Road
4608 Golf Terrace
304 Griffit Street
4215 Grimes Avenue
4222 Grimes Avenue
4223 Grimes Avenue
4226 Grimes Avenue
4231 Grimes Avenue
4232 Grimes Avenue
4235 Grimes Avenue
4238 Grimes Avenue
4239 Grimes Avenue
4242 Grimes Avenue
4247 Grimes Avenue
4306 Grimes Avenue
4407 Grimes Avenue
4412 Grimes Avenue
4503 Grimes Avenue
5417 Grove Street

5016 Halifax Avenue
5016 Hankerson Avenue
5920 Hansen Road
301 Harrison Avenue

404 Harrison Avenue
5020 Indianola Avenue
6416 Interlachen Boulevard
305 Jefferson Avenue
307 Jefferson Avenue
309 Jefferson Avenue
313 Jefferson Avenue
317 Jefferson Avenue
315 John Street
317 John Street
4238 Lynn Avenue
4240 Lynn Avenue
4242 Lynn Avenue

4387 Mackay Avenue
4390 Mackay Avenue
4394 Mackay Avenue
303 Madison Avenue
305 Madison Avenue
307 Madison Avenue
308 Madison Avenue
312 Madison Avenue
313 Madison Avenue
316 Madison Avenue
6212 Maloney Avenue
6301 Maloney Avenue
6528 Maloney Avenue
6615 Maloney Avenue

5000 Mirror Lakes Drive
6933 Moccasin Valley Road
407 Monroe Avenue
4003 Morningside Road (Morningside Congregational Church)
4101 Morningside Road
4103 Morningside Road
4107 Morningside Road
4111 Morningside Road
4211 Morningside Road
4305 Morningside Road
4307 Morningside Road
4311 Morningside Road
4313 Morningside Road
4315 Morningside Road
4401 Morningside Road
5131 Motor Street
5135 Motor Street

4425 North Avenue
4501 North Avenue
5817 Olinger Road
6232 Peacedale Avenue
6233 Peacedale Avenue
6300 Peacedale Avenue
6301 Peacedale Avenue
4421 Rutledge Avenue
4512 Rutledge Avenue
4516 Rutledge Avenue
6324 Ryan Avenue

4225 Scott Terrace
4227 Scott Terrace
4228 Scott Terrace
4230 Scott Terrace
4231 Scott Terrace
4237 Scott Terrace
4238 Scott Terrace
4241 Scott Terrace
4242 Scott Terrace
4246 Scott Terrace
4247 Scott Terrace
5020 Summit Avenue
4000 Sunnyside Road
4003 Sunnyside Road
4004 Sunnyside Road
4007 Sunnyside Road
4008 Sunnyside Road
4009 Sunnyside Road
4012 Sunnyside Road
4013 Sunnyside Road

6501 Tingdale Avenue
5205 Valley View Road
6924 Valley View Road
400 Van Buren Avenue
5533 Vernon Avenue
5721 Vernon Avenue
5912 Vernon Avenue
6417 Warren Avenue
405 Washington Avenue
407 Washington Avenue
6525 Waterman Avenue
5029 William Avenue
5033 William Avenue
6104 Wilryan Avenue
6300 Wilryan Avenue
6333 Wilryan Avenue
5909 Wooddale Avenue
4024 Woodend Drive
5832 Zenith Avenue

3916 44th Street West
3920 44th Street West
3936 44th Street West
4006 44th Street West
4010 44th Street West
4012 44th Street West
4014 44th Street West
4016 44th Street West
4018 44th Street West
4020 44th Street West
4100 44th Street West
4112 44th Street West
4116 44th Street West
4120 44th Street West
4212 44th Street West
4216 44th Street West
4217 44th Street West
4500 44th Street West
4520 44th Street West
4600 44th Street West
4101 45th Street West
4105 45th Street West
4129 45th Street West
5117 48th Street West
3945 49th Street West
5105 49th Street West
3509 54th Street West
3725 54th Street West
4529 56th Street West
4900 60th Street West
5309 60th Street West

Footnotes

Sand Castles on France Avenue: An Introduction

1. Surveyor's Field Notes for Township 28, North Range 24, West 4th Principal Meridian, Minnesota, 1853, on file at Minnesota Secretary of State's Office.
2. Jeffrey A. Hess, Interview with Aldora Cornelius Hallaway, April 18, 1979.
3. Hess, Interviews with Bill Hoffman, April 9, April 11, 1979.

From Farmyards to Backyards: A Brief History

1. According to 1960 federal census data, about 68 percent of the approximately 8,000 homes in the city postdated 1950. Since at least 4,400 new residences have been constructed since 1960 (and an unknown number of pre-1950 homes demolished), residences of post-1950 vintage account for at least 80 percent of the city's total residential structures. U. S. Bureau of the Census, *U. S. Census of Housing, 1960*, vol. 1, pt. 5 (Washington, D.C.: U. S. Government Printing Office, 1963), pp. 25-38; Jeffrey A. Hess, Interview with Robert Lunieski, Edina Assessor's Office, April 9, 1979.
2. Paul Hesterman, "History of Edina," unpublished report prepared for Edina Historical Society, n. d., p. 20.
3. Surveyor's Field Notes for Township 117, North Range 21, West 5th Principal Meridian, Minnesota, 1854; Township 28, North Range 24, West 4th Principal Meridian, Minnesota, 1853, on file at Minnesota Secretary of State's Office.
4. Hesterman, p. 9; R. Cook, *Sectional Map of Hennepin County* (St. Paul: L. Buechener, 1860).
5. Hesterman, pp. 9-10.
6. Hesterman, pp. 11-16. The schoolhouse, which is no longer extant, stood at the present site of Edina City Hall. The church building, formerly known as Trinity Chapel, and the Grange structure still survive, although neither is now located on its original site. The church, considerably remodeled, stands at 4924 France Avenue South. The Grange Hall is in Frank Tupa Park at Eden Avenue and Highway 100.
7. Hesterman, pp. 10-11; "The Church of St. Patrick, Edina, Minnesota" (n. p., n. d.). Cahill School is still extant, although it has been moved from its original location to Frank Tupa Park. See Foster W. Dunwiddie, National Register of Historic Places Inventory — Nomination Form for Cahill School, unpublished, July 2, 1970, on file at State Historic Preservation Office, Minnesota Historical Society.

8. Hesterman, pp. 6-9, 27, 30; George E. Warner and others, *History of Hennepin County and the City of Minneapolis* (Minneapolis: North Star Publishing Company, 1881), p. 216; Dunwiddie, National Register of Historic Places — Nomination Form for Grimes House, unpublished, September 15, 1975, on file at State Historic Preservation Office, Minnesota Historical Society.

9. R. J. Baldwin, "Edina," in *History of Minneapolis and Hennepin County*, vol. 2, eds. Isaac Atwater and John H. Stevens (New York and Chicago: Munsell Publishing Company, 1895), p. 1263; *Map of Ramsey and Washington Counties, with Adjacent Portions of Anoka, Dakota and Hennepin Counties in Minnesota* (Minneapolis: Warner and Foote, 1886).

10. Hesterman, p. 13; Baldwin, p. 1263.

11. Hesterman, pp. 20-21.

12. Hesterman, p. 21; E. Dudley Parsons, "Parsonalities," *Hennepin County Review*, February 8, 1940; "An Act to Provide for the Incorporation of Villages," *General Laws of the State of Minnesota Passed during the Twenty-Fourth Session of the State Legislature* (St. Paul: Pioneer Press Company, 1885), pp. 171-172.

13. Hesterman, pp. 22-25.

14. Edina Village Council Minutes, unpublished, May 9, 1904, on file at Edina City Hall; Hesterman, pp. 41-42.

15. "Nickel Limit Is Pushed Westward," *Minneapolis Journal*, April 11, 1905, p. 6. The electric streetcar line entered Edina along West 44th Street and proceeded west along the city's northern border to Hopkins. This route had originally been developed in 1881 by the Minneapolis, Lyndale and Minnetonka Railway, commonly called the "Motor Line." Providing steam-powered rail service between Minneapolis and Lake Minnetonka, the Motor Line was mainly a shuttle for vacationers. It had little impact on the residential development of Edina. When the Motor Line went out of business in 1886, its tracks ran through still-open countryside. See Stephen A. Kieffer, *Transit and the Twins* (Minneapolis: Twin City Rapid Transit Company, 1958), pp. 14-15; David A. Lanegran and Ernest R. Sandeen, *The Lake District of Minneapolis* (St. Paul: Living Historical Museum, 1979), pp. 24-26.

16. Hess, Interview with E. Dudley Parsons, Jr., May 6, 1979; Hesterman, p. 34.

17. As quoted in Hesterman, p. 40.

18. Hesterman, pp. 42-46.

19. As quoted in Hesterman, p. 46.

20. Edina Village Council Minutes, November 27, 1920; Hesterman, pp. 47-48.

21. Jeffrey A. Hess and William W. Scott, Architectural Style Map of Surviving Pre-1920 Edina Residences, unpublished, 1979, on file at Edina Historical Society.

22. Hesterman, "Suburban Growth in Edina, Minnesota, 1900-1930," unpublished, May 11, 1973, p. 21, on file at Edina Historical Society.

23. Thorpe Bros., "Country Club District" (n. p., n. d.); Hesterman, "History of Edina," pp. 50-55.

24. Hesterman, pp. 60-64.

25. Edina Village Council Minutes, August 24, 1928.

26. Hesterman, p. 58.

27. "2,000 on Hand as Home Complete Is Opened to Public," *Minneapolis Journal*, Real Estate Section, June 7, 1925, p. 1.

28. "Calvary of Cahill Grew up in Catholic Settlement," *Edina Courier*, July 20, 1967.

29. "Report Shows Village Growing at Rate of 2500 People Annually," *Edina-Morningside Courier*, December 2, 1954.

30. Edina Assessor's Office Files; U. S. Bureau of the Census, *Population, First Series, Number of Inhabitants, Minnesota* (Washington, D.C.: U. S. Government Printing Office, 1941), p. 8; U. S. Bureau of the Census, *U. S. Census of Housing, 1940*, vol. 2, pt. 3 (Washington, D.C.: U. S. Government Printing Office, 1943), p. 747.

31. Baldwin, p. 1263.

A Matter of Style: Edina's Changing Architecture

1. Dates in parentheses denote dates of original construction. Some of these dates are documented in the next chapter. Most, however, are approximations based on Edina Assessor's Office Files.

2. A brief overview of Edina's post-World War II architecture can be found in David Gebhard and Tom Martinson, *A Guide to the Architecture of Minnesota* (Minneapolis: University of Minnesota Press, 1977), pp. 120-122.

Site-Seeing: Significant Buildings and Districts

1. Foster W. Dunwiddie, National Register of Historic Places Inventory — Nomination Form for Baird House, unpublished, December 6, 1977, on file at State Historic Preservation Office, Minnesota Historical Society.

2. As quoted in Paul Hesterman, "History of Edina," unpublished report prepared for Edina Historical Society, n. d., p. 41.

3. "Eight Houses for Modern Living," *Life*, September 26, 1938, pp. 45, 56, 58-61.

4. "Building Started on Life's Model Home Designed for Blackbourns," Country Club *Crier*, January 1939, p. 2; "Life Home to Be Open to Public," *Crier*, May 1939, p. 4.

5. Dunwiddie, National Register of Historic Places Inventory — Nomination Form for Cahill School, unpublished, July 2, 1970, on file at State Historic Preservation Office, Minnesota Historical Society; "Cahill School," unpublished, n. d., on file at Edina Historical Society.

6. "Cahill School."

7. "Calvary of Cahill Grew up in Catholic Settlement," *Edina Courier*, July 20, 1967.

8. Jeffrey A. Hess, Interview with Rev. H. H. W. Egler, April 28, 1979.

9. Hess, Interview with Rudolph E. Brom, April 28, 1979; undated newspaper clipping in "Edina Historical Society Research — Mill, Schools, Churches," ed. Foster W. Dunwiddie, unpublished, February 18, 1975, on file at Edina Historical Society.

10. William W. Scott, Interview with Paul and Mary Carson, April 30, 1979.

11. Hess, Interview with Aldora Cornelius Hallaway, April 18, 1979.

12. Frank J. and Florence Mackey, Warranty Deed to Alice Dartt, September 22, 1910, Book of Deeds 683, p. 427; G. Foster Smith, Mortgage to Alice B. and George B. Dartt, September 22, 1910, on file at Hennepin County Recorder's Office; *Davison's Minneapolis Directory* (Minneapolis: Minneapolis Directory Company, 1910), p. 486.

13. Stephen A. Kieffer, *Transit and the Twins* (Minneapolis: Twin City Rapid Transit Company, 1958), pp. 31-32; Frank J. and Florence Mackey, Plat of Browndale Park, October 28, 1909, on file at Hennepin County Recorder's Office.

14. Hesterman, p. 54; Frank J. Mackey, Warranty Deed to Maud C. Dyer, October 3, 1912, Book of Deeds 728, p. 178, on file at Hennepin County Recorder's Office.

15. Conklin and Bonne Company, Mortgage to Maud C. and William C. Dyer, September 12, 1913, Book of Mortgages 781, p. 255; Mackey, Warranty Deed to Claude D. Kimball, July 10, 1912, Book of Deeds 707, p. 595; Roberts Hamilton Company *vs.* Claude D. Kimball, Lien, February 5, 1913, Book of Liens 43, p. 631; Mary A. Barber, Warranty Deed to William J. Jalley, October 24, 1912, Book of Deeds 722, p. 325; W. C. J. Hermann, Mortgage to William J. Jalley, June 14, 1913, Book of Mortgages 783, p. 190, on file at Hennepin County Recorder's Office; *Davison's Minneapolis Directory* (Minneapolis: Minneapolis Directory Company, 1912), pp. 575, 1048.

16. Hess, Interview with Jack Lovett, April 9, 1979; "Edina Baptist Grew from Lake Harriet Baptist Mission," *Edina Courier*, July 6, 1967.

17. "New Edina Theater to Go Up at 50th and France," *Crier*, April 1934, p. 4; Edina Theater File, J. J. Liebenberg Papers, on file at Northwest Architectural Archives, University of Minnesota.

18. Hess, Interview with Hazel Jackson, May 6, 1979; Massasoit Land Company, Warranty Deed to Etta Erickson, March 29, 1911, Book of Deeds 690, p. 621; Harriet G. and Charles O. Andrews, Warranty Deed to Etta Erickson, April 6, 1911, Book of Deeds 684, p. 491; Bruer Bros. Lumber Company *vs.* Etta Erickson, Lien, November 15, 1911, Book of Liens 38, p. 541, on file at Hennepin County Recorder's Office; *Davison's Minneapolis Directory* (Minneapolis: Minneapolis Directory Company, 1911), p. 587.

19. O. H. Kelley, *Origin and Progress of the Order of the Patrons of Husbandry in the United States* (Philadelphia: J. A. Wagenseller, 1875), pp. 22, 30.

20. Dunwiddie,National Register of Historic Places Inventory — Nomination Form for Grange Hall, unpublished, July 2, 1970, on file at State Historic Preservation Office, Minnesota Historical

Society; Hesterman, pp. 15-16, 28; "Minnehaha Grange Hall," unpublished, n. d., on file at Edina Historical Society.

21. "Minnehaha Grange Hall."

22. Dunwiddie, National Register of Historic Places Inventory — Nomination Form for Grimes House, unpublished, September 15, 1975, on file at State Historic Preservation Office, Minnesota Historical Society.

23. Dunwiddie, Grimes House.

24. Because of Leerskov's extensive building activities in Morningside, deed and mortgage records proved to be of little use in determining a construction date for this residence. The date of 1910 is based on Edina Assessor's Office Files and interviews with longtime Edina residents. Hess, Interview with Hazel Jackson, May 6, 1979; Hess, Interview with E. Dudley Parsons, Jr., May 6, 1979; Hesterman, pp. 43, 45, 47.

25. Hess, Interview with E. Dudley Parsons, Jr., April 30, 1979; "Pay-As-You-Go Basis at Morningside Church," *Minneapolis Journal*, December 17, 1912, p. 11.

26. "New Chapel Is Proposed," *Minneapolis Journal*, April 11, 1913, p. 13; "Tiny Chapel to Be Transformed," *Minneapolis Journal*, August 23, 1913, p. 2.

27. Hess, Interview with Edward Anderson, May 3, 1979.

28. E. D. Parsons, *Harriet News*, March 27, 1920, as quoted in Hesterman, p. 44.

29. Edina Assessor's Office Files list the date of construction for this residence as 1919, but the house was probably built a few years earlier. In 1914 Henry G. Onstad purchased the site from George and Minnie Graham. That same year, Onstad conveyed title of the property to the building contractor Niels N. Leerskov. In 1915 Leerskov returned the title to Onstad, who mortgaged the property a year later. This sequence of events suggests an approximate building date of 1915. See George and Minnie Graham, Warranty Deed to Henry G. Onstad, April 1, 1914, Book of Deeds 753, p. 583; Henry G. and Lois G. Onstad, Warranty Deed to Niels N. and Johannah M. Leerskov, October 31, 1914, Book of Deeds 767, p. 298; Niels N. and Johannah M. Leerskov, Warranty Deed to Henry G. and Lois G. Onstad, September 19, 1915, Book of Deeds 806, p. 559; David P. Jones and Company, Mortgage to Henry G. and Lois G. Onstad, September 19, 1916, Book of Mortgages 853, p. 538, on file at Hennepin County Recorder's Office.

30. J. H. Thompson, Warranty Deed to Paul Peterson, November 11, 1879, Book of Deeds 80, p. 478; J. H. Thompson, Mortgage to Paul Peterson, November 15, 1879, Book of Mortgages 55, p. 99; Paul Peterson, Affidavit, March 18, 1920, Book of Miscellaneous 1125, p. 184, on file at Hennepin County Recorder's Office; Hess, Interview with Lewis Jones, May 14, 1979.

31. Hesterman, pp. 10-11.

32. "The Church of St. Patrick, Edina, Minnesota" (n. p., 1957).

33. Jean Foster, "Irish Potato Famine Fostered First Edina Congregation," *Edina Courier*, June 22, 1967; Ray Gunter, "Edina Plans New Buildings," *Minneapolis Star*, May 9, 1963, p. 5.

34. David Gebhard and Tom Martinson, *A Guide to the Architecture of Minnesota* (Minneapolis: University of Minnesota Press, 1977), p. 122.

35. William B. and Lillian H. Riley, Plat of Riley's Subdivision of Lots 3, 4, 5, 6, 7, 30, and 31 Grimes Homestead, May 10, 1910, on file at Hennepin County Recorder's Office.

36. Riley and Riley, Warranty Deed to Alfred J. and Jessie M. Simmons, August 6, 1910, Book of Deeds 676, p. 510, on file at Hennepin County Recorder's Office.

37. *Davison's Minneapolis Directory* (Minneapolis: Minneapolis Directory Company, 1912), p. 1734; Hess, Interview with Stewart J. McIntosh, May 5, 1980.

38. Hesterman, p. 40.

39. Hess, Interview with Hazel Jackson, May 6, 1979; Edward E. Grimes and others, Warranty Deed to Iva M. Skone, August 10, 1905, Book of Deeds 594, p. 494; Ella A. Eustis, Mortgage to Iva M. and Oliver Skone, August 10, 1905, Book of Mortgages 571, p. 594; Bruer Bros. Lumber Company *vs.* Iva M. Skone, Lien, November 16, 1906, Book of Liens 20, p. 356; Alexander Hodel, Mortgage to Iva M. and Oliver Skone, October 28, 1910, Book of Mortgages 712, p. 70; Jones and Sawyer *vs.* Iva M. Skone, Lien, July 10, 1911, Book of Liens 38, p. 63; Clara E. Barnard, Mortgage to Iva M. and Oliver Skone, September 21, 1911, Book of Mortgages 737, p. 126, on file at Hennepin County Recorder's Office.

40. *Davison's Minneapolis Directory* (Minneapolis: Minneapolis Directory Company, 1907), p. 1540.

41. The exact construction date of the Sly House is unknown. In 1866 the Slys purchased their farm from James and Margaret Davis for a total of $1,750. In 1870 the federal census evaluated the Sly house at $4,800 and their land at $675. The significant increase in the farmstead's value during this four-year period suggests that the Slys either extensively remodeled the Davis dwelling or built a substantial, new structure. See Gordon W. Stuart, "Survey on the Building Known as the 'Sly House,' " unpublished report prepared for Edina Heritage Preservation Board, February 24, 1977, on file at Edina Historical Society.

42. Hesterman, p. 58.

43. "A Break-Through for Two-Level Shopping Centers," *Architectural Forum*, December 1956, p. 117.

44. *Journal of the Sixteenth Annual Council of the Diocese of Minnesota* (Minneapolis: Johnson and Smith, 1874), p. 39; Dunwiddie, "The Episcopal Church in Edina," unpublished, June 17, 1976, p. 3, on file at Edina Historical Society.

45. Dunwiddie, "Episcopal Church," p. 4.

46. Elsie VanDusen, Trinity Chapel Data Sheet, unpublished, January 5, 1942, W. P. A. Papers, Box 313, on file at Minnesota Historical Society.

47. Hesterman, p. 14.

48. Hesterman, pp. 48-49; "Four Graduates of Edina's First School Help Dedicate 2 New $215,000 Structures," *Minneapolis Journal*, December 11, 1916, p. 5; Margaret Morris, "Morningside Grew Out of 'Hole in Mud,' " *Minneapolis Star*, December 30, 1954, p. 4; "Edina's New School Dedicated Tomorrow," December 9, 1926, unidentified newspaper clipping in "Edina Historical Society Research," on file at Edina Historical Society; "School Addition Bonds Are Voted," *Crier*, November 1935, pp. 1, 18.

49. Samuel Thorpe, *Hennepin County Review*, May 25, 1922, as quoted in Hesterman, pp. 50-51.

50. Thorpe Bros., "Country Club District" (n. p., n. d.).

51. Hesterman, p. 51; Thorpe Bros., Plat of Country Club District, Brown Section, April 8, 1924; Plat of Country Club District, Fairway Section, June 4, 1924, on file at Hennepin County Recorder's Office.

52. See Thorpe Bros., Warranty Deed to William H. Korn, March 16, 1925, Book of Deeds 1042, p. 506; Warranty Deed to Guerdon J. and Fern C. Bach, October 29, 1924, Book of Deeds 1042, p. 470, on file at Hennepin County Recorder's Office.

53. Thorpe Bros., Warranty Deed to William H. Korn; Warranty Deed to Guerdon J. and Fern C. Bach. Following approved real estate practices of the time, Thorpe Bros. wrote these restrictions into all deeds conveying title to property in the Country Club District. As expressly stipulated in the deeds, all of the restrictions, with one major exception, were to expire on or before January 1, 1964. The exception concerned the clause barring non-Caucasians from owning property in the district. This restriction was to remain in force forever. In 1948, however, the United States Supreme Court invalidated all racially exclusive real estate covenants. See J. C. Nichols, "A Developer's View of Deed Restrictions," *Journal of Land and Public Utility Economics*, 5 (May 1929), 132-142; Clement E. Vose, *Caucasians Only: The Supreme Court, the NAACP, and the Restrictive Covenant Cases* (Berkeley and Los Angeles: University of California Press, 1959), pp. vii, 205-210.

54. Thorpe Bros., "Country Club."

55. June Schmidt, " 'Yes Sir, Those Country Club Houses Were Hard to Unload,' " *Edina Sun*, January 28, 1971.

56. In their project correspondence for the Country Club District, Liebenberg and Kaplan state that in 1927 they built "seven houses . . . of approximately the same size, as one operation, under one contract"; see Liebenberg and Kaplan, Letter to Charles Hay, August 6, 1932, J. J. Liebenberg Papers, on file at Northwest Architectural Archives, University of Minnesota. The Liebenberg Papers contain an annotated plat map and a

job description list which indicate that the firm in 1926-27 prepared architectural drawings for at least eight houses in the Country Club District. Seven sets of drawings survive, but only five can be matched with existing buildings. These five plans bear the following job description numbers: M381E, M382D, M376C, M373A, M375G. The two other surviving sets of plans were apparently prepared for residences at 4600 and 4613 Edina Boulevard. But these drawings do not resemble the houses occupying these sites; see 377F, 378H. The missing set of plans was apparently designed for 4606 Moorland Avenue. Since the job description list provides a project completion date for the site, it is possible that the residence at this address was built by Liebenberg and Kaplan as a model home; see 374B.

57. Hesterman, pp. 54, 65; "Sales of Country Club Real Estate Continue Steady," *Crier*, November 1936, p. 5; "Building Increases 50% in C. C. District in 12-Month Period," *Crier*, January 1937, p. 1.

58. Hesterman, p. 55.

59. Scott and Hess, Stylistic Analysis of Country Club District Architecture, unpublished, 1979, on file at Edina Historical Society.

60. "One of Our New Homes," *Crier*, October 1935, p. 4; "One of Our New Homes," *Crier*, November 1935, p. 12; "Our New December Home," *Crier*, December 1935, p. 8; "Our New Home for January," *Crier*, January 1936, p. 8; "French Simplicity Inspires This Month's New Home Selection," *Crier*, May 1936, pp. 10-11; "Home with Colonial Background Is June's New Home Selection," *Crier*, June 1936, pp. 10-11; "New American Home Framework Finished at 4807 Sunnyside," *Crier*, August 1936, p. 1; Hess, Interview with Liebenberg, April 18, 1978.

61. Gebhard and Martinson, p. 120.

62. Thorpe Bros., Plat of Brucewood, August 4, 1938; Plat of Country Club District, Sunny Slope Section, August 10, 1939; Carl M. Hansen and Ben M. Parks, Plat of Hansen and Parks's First Addition, Country Club District, May 3, 1937; Annabel Mae and Merril Hutchinson, Plat of Hilldale, July 10, 1939; Plat of Rolling Green, August 24, 1936; George A. and Casimira Specht, Plat of South White Oaks Addition, May 10, 1939; J. Frank and Catherine T. Ecklund, Plat of White Oaks, May 1, 1937; Plats of White Oaks, Second-Fifth Additions, May 2-October 10, 1938, on file at Hennepin County Recorder's Office.

63. *1939 Directory of Metropolitan Edina* (Hopkins: The Country Club Crier, 1939).

64. See Don Riddle, "Homes to Last for All Time," *National Real Estate Journal*, March 4, 1929, pp. 22-28; "Building Homes by the Block to Sell a New Development," *National Real Estate Journal*, March 18, 1929, pp. 52-58; Frederick Law Olmsted, "Palos Verdes Estates," *Landscape Architecture*, 17 (July 1927), 255-279; Henry V. Hubbard, "The Golf Course and the Land Subdivision," *Landscape Architecture*, 17 (April 1927), 211-219.

65. Thorpe Bros., "Country Club District."

66. "Nickel Limit is Pushed Westward," *Minneapolis Journal*, April 11, 1905, p. 6; Edward Grimes and others, Plat of Morningside, June 17, 1905; Plat of Grimes Homestead, May 5, 1906; Crocker and Crowells' First Addition, June 28, 1907; Clarence F. Williams and others, Plat of Berkeley Heights, June 11, 1910; William B. and Lillian H. Riley, Plat of Riley's Subdivision of Lots 3, 4, 5, 6, 7, 30, and 31 Grimes Homestead, May 10, 1910, on file at Hennepin County Recorder's Office.

67. Hesterman, p. 34; Hess, Interview with E. Dudley Parsons, Jr., May 6, 1979.

68. Hess and Scott, Architectural Style Map of Surviving pre-1920 Edina Residences, unpublished, 1979, on file at Edina Historical Society.

69. Norman Francis Thomas, *Minneapolis-Moline: A History of Its Formation and Operation* (New York: Arno Press, 1976), p. 196; *Map of West Minneapolis and Surrounding Country* (Minneapolis: A. Hageboeck, n. d.); Charles P. and Mary A. Silloway, Plat of West Minneapolis Heights, July 26, 1887, on file at Hennepin County Recorder's Office; *Minneapolis City Directory* (Minneapolis: Harrison and Smith, 1886), p. 707.

70. See Hess and Scott, West Minneapolis Heights Data Cards, unpublished, 1979, on file at Edina Historical Society; P. M. Dahl, *Plat Book of Hennepin County Minnesota* (Minneapolis: Northwestern Map Publishing Company, 1898), p. 30.

Credits

Calvary Lutheran Church, p. 38 (above).
Foster W. Dunwiddie, p. 9.
Edina Historical Society, pp. 1-4, 7-8, 12-14, 18 (above), 34 (above), 37 (below), 41 (below), 45 (above), 48 (below), 51 (above), 55 (above), 64-66.
Jeffrey A. Hess, pp. 5, 18 (below), 49.
Stewart J. and Ruth McIntosh, p. 56 (above).
Minneapolis Public Library, p. 15.
Minnehaha Grange No. 398, pp. 6, 34 (below), 47 (below).
Minnesota Historical Society, pp. 10-11, 44 (above).
Minnesota Secretary of State's Office, p. xi.
Setter, Leach & Lindstrom, Inc., pp. 16-17, 19-29, 31, 35-36, 37 (above), 38 (below), 39-40, 41 (above), 42-43, 44 (below), 45 (below), 46, 47 (above), 48 (above), 50, 51 (below), 52-54, 55 (below), 56 (below), 57-61, 67, 69, 71.

Index of Names and Places

Numbers in bold indicate illustrations.

Index of Addresses

General street references are included in the following list. Numbers in bold indicate illustrations.

Authors

William W. Scott, A.I.A., is vice-president of Setter, Leach & Lindstrom, Inc. A recognized authority in the field of preservation architecture, Scott has served as chairman of the Minneapolis Heritage Commission and as state preservation coordinator for the American Institute of Architects. He makes his home in Taylors Falls, Minnesota, where he has restored an 1857 Greek Revival residence.

Jeffrey A. Hess is a free-lance writer and historical consultant based in Minneapolis. As a Woodrow Wilson Fellow and a Kent Fellow, Hess received advanced degrees in English and American Civilization from Brown University. His historical writings have appeared in *American Quarterly, Rhode Island History, Yankee Magazine,* and publications of the Minnesota Historical Society.